CW01642437

RECYCLE ANGEL

RECYCLE ANGEL

Fred Page

ISBN 978-1-3999-1259-4

This is a work of fiction. Names, characters, places, and incidents either are the product of the author's imagination or are used fictitiously. Any resemblance to actual persons, living or dead, events, or locales is entirely coincidental.

Copyright © 2021 by Fred Page

All rights reserved. No part of this book may be reproduced or used in any manner without written permission of the copyright owner except for the use of quotations in a book review.

For more information, contact:
recycle.angel26@gmail.com

Published by Fred Page
fredpageauthor.co.uk

Cover design by Natalie Grainger

I am pleased to dedicate this book to my dad, Debbie, Judy and Natalie.

My dad will be looking down from heaven and laughing that I based Granddad, the fun, mischievous character who always gets his own way, on him. He would have approved of my light hearted approach to problem solving because he knew me so well.

In writing this story I learned it would not have been possible without Debbie's patience, Judy's editing and Natalie's graphic skills. I can't imagine anyone ever had a better more supportive team and without them this book would never have left the office.

Now my tinkering is finished, I can thank them, tell them it has been a pleasure working with them and hope they are looking forward to the next story.

CONTENTS

CHAPTER 1

GRANDDAD plonked something on the kitchen worktop and asked "What is that?"

Whatever it was it appeared to be laminated.

He stared defiantly at the thing then at me until I picked it up and examined it. "Hand written note" I observed. "Where did you find it?"

He almost grumbled, "In the bin".

"In the bin" I grumbled back. "Why did you take it out?"

He didn't answer my question. He had one of his own. "It was stuck in the bin. Stuck to the lid. Could have been there for years and I've just found it. Have you got one?"

I wondered why I should. I hadn't looked in the bin recently so couldn't really say. Before he told me to look, I volunteered. I thought there are only three bins, I will look in all of them but Granddad followed me and shouted "The blue bin FREDDY!"

I complained to myself he could have asked his neighbours. He always asks me the silly questions because he knows I will do whatever he asks and I wont complain. Holding the bin handles I asked, sort of accusingly, "This one? Do you want to look?"

He stood and stared. He didn't have to tell me, I had to do it. Teasing, I lifted the lid slowly, a little at a time until he shouted, "That's it!"

I did not expect to see it, in fact I hoped I wouldn't. Disappointed, I saw the note or poster whatever it was and I felt my shoulders droop knowing I would have to read it. I pulled it and said, "Let's take it inside".

We compared the hand writing and agreed it was the same on both posters.

Granddad remembered at school he was given lines to write for misbehaving and said, "This child must have been really bad".

"It is a list" I told him, "Look! Cardboard, cans, tins, jars, bottles, plastics. A list of things to put in the Recycling bin. What else could it be?"

I surprised myself, I said, "I always wanted a list like this. It could be really useful".

Granddad smiled. He had found something useful and was pleased with himself. "Really useful?" he asked. "Why?"

I had never been sure what can be recycled and this list would help. Luckily I clean my recyclables and horde them until the Bin Men are due, and had a tray full in the cupboard. We could use them to practice and work out how to use it? With the tray on the worktop I brushed my hand over everything and told Granddad it was supposed to be ready to be put in the Recycling bin but to test the list we would not assume I had got it right. We had to check everything.

"If we can't assume anything," Granddad said, "tell me what are we looking for?"

I began at the beginning and told him recycling started in America. The Americans made so much rubbish they had to find a way to stop America becoming a Dump. A young American boy drew the Reduce, Reuse and Recycle symbol, three arrows going round in a circle. I claimed it is stamped on everything that can be recycled.

I suggested we could pretend to be Americans but Granddad huffed, "Let's not! We can be the best of British, if you don't mind". I shrugged and he questioned reduce, reuse and recycle and told me he knew the first two.

In my poshest English voice I asked him to think of things he could reduce?

In his poshest English voice he said water, wood, steel, glass, almost anything. Having practiced reducing all his life he was an expert, he had learned it is a good way to save. He said, “If you boil just enough water for two cups of tea, one for you and one for me, you will save water, electricity and money”. He had come prepared. He had brought a cup with the logo, Recycle Angel, and put it on the worktop. “My cup!” he said sternly. “And when you are ready, we can have a nice cup of tea”.

Filling the kettle and switching it on to boil I bragged, “After years of practice I usually guess right. Watch me!”

“Go on then!” Granddad grinned and challenged “prove it!”

I accepted his challenge, put tea bags in his cup and my Old Codger one and with every drop of water made the tea. Before I could stop him Granddad reached out and took his Recycle Angel cup and left me the Old Codger one. I wanted him to swap, but he wouldn’t. Instead, to cheer me up, he told me he will be a Recycle Angel when I have taught him everything I know. I felt flattered but doubted I know enough and said, “We’ll see”.

The aim of recycling is to find stuff the Council know can be sorted and sold to make something new. The label, symbol and instructions on packaging are clues but of course we have to make up our minds to put each item in the blue Recycling Bin or the khaki General Waste one. I took a red can and asked Granddad to look for the sign and tag the can blue or khaki.

He pressed it into my hand saying, “Small print!”

Realising the print was small and hard to read I said, “Hot potato” and gave it back to him. He studied the print more carefully, spotted the symbol and cheered, “There it is!”

Together we examined it, and the instruction below it which read, 100% recyclable. He concluded it could be tagged blue.

Turning the can in my hand, being more diligent than usual, I noticed another symbol, a single arrow circle with the instructions, widely recyclable.

"Only widely recyclable" I complained and asked myself, does that mean it isn't always recycled? Might the Council not want it? I asked Granddad what he thought? He didn't know and asked me then irritatingly argued the Council would take it. He made me feel silly and should agree when he said, "You know what I mean, Freddy?"

I didn't agree. I felt the Council may be clever, but not infallible and neither are we. We had tagged the red can blue but now I wondered if it should be khaki. Annoyed I responded and to irritate him said, "Very helpful! I knew that! You know what I mean!"

Drinking tea and reflecting on our conversation I noticed my list. Trying not to be noticed I glanced at it and saw the word can. Grandad was right, the Council wanted it. Embarrassed I laughed, "Silly me, cans are on the list".

Pleased with himself Granddad grinned. He wanted to carry on tagging anything and everything and picked a lemonade bottle from the tray. Shocked to find it was light he commented, "Not very heavy this one, made of cheap glass". I explained bottles used to be heavy because they were made of glass, but now they are made of plastic. That is why it was light.

He didn't listen. He said, "I knew that" and began hunting for clues. He checked the top, bottom and label, found what he was looking for and showed me. We talked about it and I told him some plastic can be recycled and some can't and asked him to tell me what sort of plastic it is?

He sat up straight and with an air of superiority said, "What do you mean, what sort of plastic? It is the sort that is widely recycled, it says so. And before you ask, bottles are on the list". He had been thorough. He was right. I grimaced and asked him again what sort of plastic but he insisted he didn't need to know. He glibly told me not to worry, bottles are on the list and we should tag it blue and put it in the blue bin.

There were lots of other things on the tray and I smugly told myself making decisions about some might be harder. He picked a large cereal box. Determined to find the sign or discard it as rubbish he turned it, found the widely recycled information, checked the list, and as expected, announced it should be tagged blue. He impressed me. He had a talent for spotting the clues and making decisions.

"Tea?" I asked and filled the kettle, flicked the switch and put tea bags in the cups. He watched me and muttered, "I could do that". When the water boiled the kettle rattled and steamed he told me it was boiling and when I scalded the tea bags in the cups and added the milk he didn't say he could do it but cheekily commented, "Making tea is so easy. Anyone can do it".

I realised that was a hint to let him do it. We smiled at each other and I gave him a cheeky reply, "I might let you".

Keen to get on and learn more and assure himself he understood the symbols, signs and anything else, he picked up one of those every-day parcel brown cardboard boxes and turned it over and over. He could not find a symbol or sign or information. He looked puzzled and asked for my advice.

"Cardboard box" I told him. "I put one of these in my blue bin when it was new. It was the first thing I put in it. They are never stamped, signed, have no symbol or instructions but always recycled. Cardboard is on the list, so don't worry".

It annoyed Granddad. He had developed a good check top, bottom and label routine to find clues so when he didn't find any he protested he might have put it in the khaki bin, if I hadn't told him. He stressed others might have made the same mistake. In his opinion that would be a terrible waste, and he wondered if we could do something to help the others?

We were working together, doing our best, not experts but getting better. To help others we would have to know it all, however, I could not resist asking if he thought he was on the way to becoming a true Recycle Angel?

He looked thoughtfully at the tray and said, "I am having fun Freddy. It takes me some time to see what I'm looking for. If I was like you, younger and could see better it would be easier. I thought I was flying but now know I need a bit more practice. I will get there".

I seemed to have more confidence in him than he did. I could see he wanted to improve. He had potential.

Looking down on the tray I could see he was counting and asked him why?

"Lots of cardboard" he told me. "It is very popular".

My view is cardboard is far too popular. It irritates me, I think we cut down too many trees just so we can have paper and cardboard. I told him we need paper and cardboard to be recycled to save the trees! I had tried to hide my annoyance, however, the look on his face told me he realised how I felt. He solemnly said, "Listen to me. Do not expect things to be the way you want them to be. Accept them as they are". He spoke slowly and considering every word said, "We need trees, paper and cardboard. We will put this tray full of stuff in your blue bin".

Wishing to save the trees as quickly as possible, I picked up the tray and was about to do what he said. He stopped me, told he wanted to know what the Council does with the stuff and we could put that stuff in the blue bin later.

I only really knew the Council collects my recycling in the Recycling Wagon and takes it somewhere to be made into something new, but I had heard bottles are smashed into pieces and made into a few things such as new bottles, insulation or used to build roads. I told Granddad. He applauded and grinned. He said, "Recycled glass can be made into all those things? I like recycling".

I knew recycling was useful but I had never thought too much about it and Granddad's reaction made me wonder what else I knew. On the tray I saw glass bottles and jars, cans, tins, plastic milk bottles and lots of cardboard. Pointing I explained milk bottles are often made into new milk bottles, cans into new cans, tins into new tins and "Cardboard…"

Before I finished Granddad laughed, "Can be made into boxes".

"It can be made into other things too" I told him, "plaster board, chipboard, paper bags, towels, tissues and more. It is very useful".

Granddad was getting more interested in recycling and wanted to know why the American boy had invented the three arrows in a circle symbol? I told him "I don't know, but since he did we've all been going round in circles trying to save the Planet". He laughed and so did I. Talking to him about recycling made it more fun, enjoyable, interesting than I ever thought it could be. I concluded, "So there you are! You know as much as I do. Did you find that interesting?"

He admitted he had never realised how useful waste stuff can be. In future he would always hunt for the clues and collect all the recycling.

His interest in recycling had grown and he wanted me to tell him about the Recycling Wagon and the Bin Men? I corrected him. "Bin men and women" I said, "and they are all Operatives".

Granddad said, "I would like to see the Operatives working, emptying bins. I have seen them but never watched them. I think it will be interesting".

"You're in luck!" I exclaimed. "They are due later today! We can put that stuff in the blue bin, put the bin out and watch. Come on!"

"Watch? Later?" Granddad muttered. "Will we have time for another cuppa?"

"Go on" I said, "you can make it, but I want your cup. While you make the tea I will do those jobs then try to explain how the recycling wagon works".

I'd seen it hundreds of times and even watched my bins being emptied a couple of times. Unsure where to begin I described the wagon as a huge tank on wheels with an hydraulic arm on the back. I told him the Operatives wheel the bins and push lots of buttons. The first one makes the arm grab the bin. The next one twists and turns it upside down so it empties into the tank. They push another one and the arm twists and turns the bin the right way up and lowers it to the ground. The last one is the let-go button and the arm releases the bin so the Operatives can wheel it back on to the pavement and go. I rounded off with, "It is unbelievably easy. When they have finished I wheel the empty bin back into the car port".

Granddad followed my description. Like an hydraulic arm he wriggled and twisted and assured me he understood.

"That's good" I told him, "because the hydraulic arm does its job and a huge paddle scraper clears up the mess". This time, with one arm I demonstrated the lift, twist and lowering of an imaginary bin and at the same time rolled my other arm round like a paddle.

Granddad congratulated me and observed, "Pulling bins and pushing buttons. The Council has made the Operative's job so much easier".

His response made me feel he understood as much as possible, and I congratulated myself for having done such a great job. "It is easy," I said smugly. "The Operatives only take half a minute to empty the bins, leave them to be collected and move on to the next house".

Granddad commentated as he copied my arm lifting and twisting movements in a ridiculous fashion and grinned, "That is fascinating!"

I tried to hide the satisfaction I felt with a modest smile. He looked me in the eye and I expected more praise. He grinned and repeated my description of Operatives pulling bins and pushing buttons then said, "You must be joking".

I had tried and failed to describe something I honestly know nothing about.

Granddad used to be a Bin Man before he retired. Council did not have wheelie bins, Operatives or Recycling Wagons. He used to lift bins and obviously found it hard to believe Operatives do so much button pushing. I told myself things have changed, bins are bigger, machines are cleverer and it occurred to me Operatives might not push so many buttons, one might be enough. The best way for him to learn would be to watch the Recycling Wagon. He would see the new ways and learn new tricks. This would be an experience of a lifetime for him.

We seemed to wait a very long time for the wagon, but we were ready when it arrived. We watched the Operatives wheel the neighbour's bin into line with mine, push them against the wagon, and press a button. In an amazing top speed synchronised thirty-second bin emptying performance the two bins were lifted, emptied and placed on the ground. Finally the Operatives grabbed them and wheeled them onto the path, then raced down the road to empty the next ones.

I wondered how much Granddad had learned? He saw the wagon, the Operatives, the bins doing back flips and it was all over in the blink of an eye. The fastest thirty-seconds of his life. The whole thing had been a blur. He seemed to be dazed and asked, "What happened?"

I gave the only answer possible, "They emptied the bins".

Determined to recall every detail, he described what he could and drew pictures in the air. He had not noticed the huge rotating scraper so I reminded him if it didn't sweep the waste into the tank there would be recycling waste everywhere. I reminded him mine will have been scraped, squashed and jumbled with all the rest, to make the back of the wagon tidy, and be on its way to be sorted.

Granddad looked into the air, as if trying to remember something then asked, "Sorted? What do you mean sorted?"

CHAPTER 2

We were entering more unknown territory. I didn't know what I meant by sorted. They say if you speak to enough people you will eventually speak to the right one. I didn't know where to call or who to ask but made several phone calls. With each one I learned a little bit more and discovered no one is interested in beginners. Finally I talked to Joe, the manager of the local MATERIAL RECOVERY FACILITY, the MRF. I told him a little white lie. I said we were Recycling Experts and would love to visit his Facility. I promised we would not ask any awkward questions so would be no trouble. He said OK.

Pleased with myself I rushed to tell Granddad the exciting news. "Granddad! Tomorrow we are going to the Material Recovery Facility. The place where Council take all the stuff to be sorted".

I told him about all my phone calls, my conversation with Joe and how I misled him into believing we are experts in recycling. He laughed when I said I told Joe we wouldn't ask any awkward questions then frowned and pointed out he might ask us a few. We would go tomorrow and pretend we are experts and if he asked questions and we didn't know the answers he would realise we were imposters. In panic I asked what we could do. Granddad answered, "We should learn as much as possible, build our confidence and be ready". He announced, "Tomorrow we will be experts!"

I squealed nervously, "I don't think I know enough, I don't feel confident! What can we do?"

Granddad had a theory. If I kept talking and learning I might not panic.

He suggested I could give him a lesson. We could learn together.

I had done my exams at school with good results. Granddad had no good results but had a talent for making things up and getting his own way. When I was ten years old he told me he had worked hard in school and been given the seat at the back of his class. I believed him until years later I went to the same school. I didn't work hard but had to sit in Granddad's old seat because alphabetically mine was the last name on the school register.

Prepared for the lesson Granddad sat on the stool at the breakfast bar. Wearing his old fashioned prescription glasses, sitting up straight, note book, pencil and wooden ruler at the ready, he looked the model student. I almost laughed when he asked, "Will this do?"

My star pupil would have earned points for good posture and looked better prepared for this lesson than me. I would have happily changed roles, he could be teacher and I could be the learner, but we had to get on with it.

My recycling tray was empty, I needed to improvise so looked round the room and then in the fridge for anything I could use. I thanked heaven when I saw a red can. We had tagged the last red can blue but that would not be enough. Joe might want more information. He might ask what the can is made of. This would be a different game.

Granddad began to measure the can and told me it was four inches high. I gave him a modern plastic ruler. It measured ten centimetres.

"It is a soft drink can" I told him, "and it is made of aluminium". While he wrote ten centimetres, red and aluminium in his book I told him red cans are very popular but not all cans are red. They are ten centimetres tall but scraped in and out of the recycling wagon on the way to the MRF they will all be squashed and crumpled. When they arrive at the MRF they will be misshapen and definitely not like new. I said, "We should expect to see hundreds of them".

With a quizzical look, he put down his pencil, picked up the can and asked, "Will we really see hundreds?"

I felt certain it is the world's favourite soft drink and just about everyone recycles the cans, so with some confidence assured him, "Hundreds or even thousands. It really is popular".

He rolled the can in his hand, found the instructions and recycling symbol but nothing to say what it was made of. He asked, "How do you know it is made of aluminium, Freddy?"

I said to myself, everybody knows that! It must be written on the can! I looked but could not find it so told him honestly, I didn't know.

Granddad did not want to assume anything so I showed him how to use Google on my phone. He Googled soft drinks cans and found they are made of aluminium. Other evidence showed it is cheaper to make new cans from old so recycling saves money.

Joking I suggested antique cans might be worth a lot of money, but doubted anyone would have one, so Granddad searched the internet.

While he did I boasted "I have recycled hundreds of them. They will have been made into new ones. If making new from old saves money, I will have saved someone a fortune".

Granddad looked at me and grinned for a long time without saying anything, then as if asking a question said, "Someone?"

I didn't know what he meant so waited for him to explain. "You!" he exclaimed. "Cheaper cans means cheaper drinks, so you have saved yourself a fortune".

With an embarrassed laugh, insisting we must get on, I took three soft drinks bottles out of the fridge and asked him to tell me if he would tag them blue or khaki?

He observed, "One big bottle and two small ones. I'll check and let you know".

Inspecting the big bottle first, he read the label, squashed it, checked the list and exasperated muttered, "Useless! There is no useful information on the label or anywhere else. Bottles are on the list so it can be recycled, but I am not happy. I don't know what it is made of" and put that bottle to one side.

The other two bottles had lots of information on the labels so I encouraged him to read them and tag them.

"Two little ones" he observed, "One has a green lid and the other is blue. I'll check the green one, first".

I crossed my fingers and wished him luck.

He squashed it, checked the top and bottom, read the label and smiled. He appeared to be pleased and when I asked why, he cleared his throat and read out "Bottle PET, cap HDPE and label PP".

"That's useful" I said, almost sarcastically, "Do you know what it means?"

Granddad took my phone and answered, "It means I can look it up, of course!"

He Googled PET and PP and learned PET can be recycled but PP cannot. Smiling he said, "We will put the bottle in the recycling and…"

Before he finished I interrupted, and in my best, clearest voice demanded, "PET can be recycled in the blue bin but I never put tops, caps or stoppers in the recycling no matter what they are made from. I am not going to make an exception for this one".

“Exactly!” Grandad exclaimed, “Just what I was going to say. The list does say bottles. It doesn’t say lids or labels! We don’t need to make any new rules, do we?” He finished, “Throw the lid and label in the bin”.

The other bottle had a blue lid and when he picked it up he almost sang “Blue lid, blue bin”.

His tone told me he was joking but just in case I advised him, “Don’t make any judgement based on the colour, Granddad. You need all the evidence to get it right”.

He followed his routine, checked the top, bottom and the label. He had found the information he wanted and put the bottle close to me. He declared, “It is made from PET, and the label states it can be recycled!” He pointed to a single arrow symbol and asked, “Tell me again what it means?”

I recited the instruction, ‘widely recycled’. He remembered and as before said, “We think it means recyclable, don’t we?”

Keen that as much as possible should be recycled Granddad praised the labelling, voted it the best he had ever seen and announced “This is what recycling is all about. It is 100% recyclable! This is top to bottom blue”. I felt an argument coming on. Firmly I said, “No matter what colour, the lid goes in the khaki bin!”

He argued, that on the label it requests, please recycle and implored, “We can’t ignore such a polite request. Can we?”

I answered loudly, “Lids!” then called, “Come on. Here is a small beans tin. Is it recyclable or rubbish, blue of khaki?”

We had put lots of tins in the Recycling bin so he could have assumed they are recyclable, but he needed to be professional.

Pretending to be an expert he carefully looked for clues on the top and bottom and the label. He found the information on the label, 'CAN METAL widely recycled' and respectfully asked my opinion.

I told him not to be confused. The can is a tin and the metal is steel and steel is recyclable and it is magnetic. I suggested he could look it up on the internet and just for fun showed him how a fridge magnet sticks to it. He took my phone and searched for tins and steel and found they can be recycled. We agreed the tin could be tagged blue. I was beginning to feel more confident I would be able to answer some questions if Joe asked.

CHAPTER 3

Now for the hard jobs! I handed Granddad an empty hot chocolate tub and warned him it might not be so easy. I told him I would have thrown it out, but kept it for something or other. The chocolate brown label had pictures of a creamy arrow and someone putting something in a bin. I hadn't seen anything like it before and had no idea what it meant. Granddad loosened the chocolate brown lid, put it aside, then sniffed inside. It distracted him. He said, "I like chocolate. I gave you lots of chocolate Freddy when you were a boy".

When I was ten, he used to give me a bar of chocolate every time I went out to play. I went out to play a lot.

He smiled, obviously thinking about the many bars of chocolate he gave me, and forgot his routine. Instead of checking the bottom of the tub he looked at the puzzling signs on the label and asked for advice. Playing detective, viewing the label with an imaginary magnifying glass, moving it up and down, pretending to bring the picture into clear view, then holding it steady joked, "We must put this in the chocolate bin".

Without thinking, Granddad naively asked, "Do you have a chocolate bin, Freddy?"

Continuing my detective role I adjusted my glasses and said, "We will have to work it out. I will test it".

He seemed to expect me to do a complicated scientific test and enthusiastically cheered, "Go on! Test it!"

There is no better test than reading the label. If you can't understand the symbols or the text it is a problem. Neither of us knew what the symbols meant. I honestly had no idea what else to do. Granddad wanted to see me do something so I told him I would do the 'thumb test'. Pressing tightly with my thumb I made a depression in the plastic and as if I had discovered something important cheered "Eureka! See that!".

Staring at my thumb gripping the plastic he grumbled, "That dent is because you are pushing it Freddy. Let go and it might pop out".

Obviously it would, as he said, pop out. I continued to play act to give the impression I knew what I was doing and told him that would prove it is made of plastic.

Granddad laughed, "You can stop pretending, stop being the very clever detective. I know it is made of plastic. I don't know what sort and if it can be recycled".

I had questioned him earlier and pressed him to tell me what sort of plastic the lemonade bottle was made of. It was his turn. He had seen through my silly game, realised it will pop out and whatever I did wouldn't show what sort of plastic it was made of. Meekly I said, "It's like milk bottles, isn't it?"

Ignoring the comparison Granddad responded, "Definitely plastic, but what sort of plastic? That is the question?"

I played with it, turned it round and round in my hand hoping for inspiration. Feeling cross I sniffed the chocolate then turned it up-side down. Stamped into the plastic was an arrow in a triangle and the letters, HDPE. I reminded myself Granddad had mentioned HDPE. I told myself it must mean something, and Googled it. The website gave lots of information and most important of all, stated it can be recycled! I still had to be convinced and argued chocolate tubs are not on the list. Granddad argued they must be. He couldn't find tub, but after trawling his finger down the list several times argued it is a pot made of HDPE plastic. He won the argument, I agreed to call it a pot and tagged it blue.

"OK!" I said, "A pot made of HDPE with a big hot chocolate coloured lid".

He chuckled, "You don't put lids in the recycling, do you Freddy? I'll put the lid in the bin and the pot… on the tray". He then announced, with great pride, "The Recycle Mystery is solved. The lid goes in the khaki bin and the pot goes in the blue one".

We had worked as a detective team and solved the chocolate pot mystery. He deserved my praise, however, he praised me. "We worked together" he insisted, "We solved the mystery and should celebrate with another cup of tea".

No time to stop. To keep up the pressure I looked in the fridge and found pots of yogurt. We had talked about pots, and through his careful detective work and understanding that the Council say pot when I say tub, he saved the chocolate one from the khaki bin. He was my chocolate pot hero. Holding up a yoghurt pot, emphasising the word pot, I asked, "Can I put this pot in the Recycling bin?"

He laughed.

I shouted "Come on Granddad. Take a look!"

He fiddled with it, turned it upside down and spun it round several times. After a while, thinking he should have found something, but suspecting he had not, I insisted he should tell me what he knew. He pointed to an arrow and some writing and told me it said check this and check that. He laughed and read the last instruction, 'check locally for kerbside'.

"That is a strange word" I told him. "I think it means the pavement. Not many people will know what it means and looking at the labelling even less people will know if this pot can be recycled". I worked out it was made of plastic, but couldn't find out what sort of plastic. Half joking Granddad said, "I think they do not know and neither do we. I feel they want this to be put in the blue bin but the instructions are potty, the label is a puzzle and I can't work out the clues. It is annoying and I want to throw it out. What should we do, Freddy?"

I had to be honest. "We don't know what to do, do we? The thing is obviously made of plastic. Is it recyclable or not recyclable? It seems unreasonable to do anything until we have discussed the clues properly. Let's pretend we are foreign and don't speak very good English. Look at the evidence, read the label, but we will not make a hasty decision". Granddad had made up his mind so pretending to agree said, "We must do everything we can". He did one of those stop for effect things then added, "Then throw it out".

To give it a chance we checked the top and bottom, reread the label and agreed to discuss our options again. It didn't take long.

Granddad said, "Yoghurt pot".

I said, "Plastic pot". We looked at each other and I said, "Excuse me saying this, but the rest is rubbish! I suggest sending the pot back to the factory and tell them to write the instructions properly".

Granddad approved. "No matter how much you like that brand, if they don't get the labelling right, buy a different brand, one that can speak plain English".

I looked in the fridge, there were a few more pots, too many to throw away. I argued, "I like the brand but not the tubs so will eat the yogurt I have, bin the pots and in future, will only buy yoghurt in pots that can be recycled. It might seem extreme but it is in a good cause so I will do it".

Granddad looked up at me with an impudent grin that made me giggle, then confirmed, "Yes you will!"

When we started looking to see what can be recycled I imagined everything would be labelled and signed and it would be easy to tag stuff blue or khaki. Neither of us thought we might consider throwing anything away. Granddad declared, "This has been a very useful exercise. We have spent a lot of time discussing pots. After a long debate we are sure it is right to tag the chocolate pot blue and the yoghurt one khaki. If we can't understand the symbols or text it is a problem and I don't recycle problems".

Granddad toyed with his pencil and complained he couldn't decide what to write. A moment later he looked up and chuckled. The idea came to him that if the best brains in Britain looked at this they would be as confused as we are, but he didn't write that. He wanted to write something that would remind him of what we had agreed. It was obvious we both thought things need to be improved. He wrote the heading POTS and a reminder to 'check pots in the shops' then mischievously asked, "Should I call them pots or tubs? I don't know".

My answer was as unhelpful as his question. "Yes, yoghurt pots sounds good, but when they are empty I'll call them tubs. You can call them what you like!"

He scribbled something so I commented, "I expect you'll have some interesting notes on pots, Grandad," but he didn't reply so I reviewed what we had found so far. "We are confident ALUMINIUM, HDPE and PET plastic can be recycled so we are making progress".

Still concerned there may be things we didn't know, signs we didn't understand, Granddad insisted, "We must sort this out! We can do it! We'll show them!"

I said to myself, many have tried and many have failed, I am one of them. However if we try together we might succeed. I cheered, "Never give up, Granddad. Everyone seems to be trying but not quite getting it together. As I said, going round in circles, but if you want to try I will help".

Granddad stopped writing his notes. I grinned, he had written a very interesting comment, 'one for the bin'. I was sure he would remember that.

All this talk about pots made me think about tea. I said, "Talking about pots! Let's stop and have a pot of tea!"

With his cup of tea steaming Granddad reminisced about the old days.

He rarely talked frankly about his experiences in the World Wars. They were bad, however when he said nothing could be so bad I disagreed.

"Hold on" I said, "we have to fight Global Warming!"

Surprised, he asked "Global what? What is that and why are we fighting it?"

Without explaining properly I told him Global Warming means the World is getting hotter. If we don't want it to overheat we have to be sensible, stop being wasteful, reduce, reuse and recycle. If we don't, the World will get too hot.

He looked doubtful so I told him we have all doubted it for too long. Now we have awful weather, storms, floods and heat waves, people are dying and being made homeless. It has to stop! "Recycling properly will help to fight it!"

He had fought in the World Wars and saved his country from oppression, misery and injustice. Keen to save his country and the World from disaster, bursting with enthusiasm he declared, "I will fight it!"

His enthusiasm encouraged me to declare, "We will fight together!" then, like a general leading his troupes into battle, shouted, "Into battle we will go". I proclaimed "Thank you Granddad. You are my inspiration, you have changed my life!" It was hard to describe what a difference he had made.

Without him I would never have thought about going to the MRF and now I thought it would be an adventure.

Joking I said, “It is hard to imagine anyone wants to buy rubbish but the MRF must sell loads of it”.

Granddad didn’t get the joke and protested “All that stuff we put in the blue bin can be recycled into something useful. It is not rubbish!”

I humbly bent my head, read the list and realised I had made lots of mistakes in the past. Some of the stuff I had put in the blue bin was rubbish. The list read only bottles and jars and I had put window glass, glass shelving, light bulbs, vases, mirrors almost anything made of glass in the blue bin. I wanted to trick Granddad so asked him to tell me everything he could think of made of glass and then asked him if it could all be recycled? He told me bottles, jars and all the things that should not be recycled, including my pyrex cup. I pretended to be impressed and congratulated him for knowing so many then, with a grin asked, “Can we tag them all blue and put them in the Recycling bin?”

With a grin he told me he would think about it and let me know. After a moments thought he worked out most of it is junk and told me only glass bottles and jars can be recycled and the rest should be put in the khaki bin.

CHAPTER 4

With a very special day ahead, instead of sleeping, I rolled about in bed worrying Granddad might not turn up and worse, I would have to make polite conversation to stop Joe asking awkward questions. My brain had just emptied and I probably snored twice before someone hammered on the door and woke me. The alarm had not gone off, but only half conscious, I turned it off. Still in my pyjamas I ran down stairs and opened the door. Granddad had arrived early. I felt flustered and had nothing organised so to give the impression things were under control uttered, "Just about to..." then realised I had no idea what I was about to do so urged him to make the tea while I dressed and had breakfast.

He gave the impression we had lots of time and yet urgently wanted a cup of tea before we left. I told myself singing is a great way to relax, no need to panic, and while he poured the tea I sang 'Tea for two'.

Sitting on the kitchen stool Granddad sipped his tea with his eyes closed and whispered, "Joe will sense something if we are stressed". I thought he had fallen asleep so was surprised when he opened his eyes and loudly, over enthusiastically said, "A nice cup of tea sets me up for the day!" then closed his eyes again.

He didn't see me rushing to get ready and didn't open his eyes again until I shouted, "Come on!"

Over relaxed, he replied, "No rush, plenty of time".

I knew it is essential to set off before the rush hour because there is always a lot of traffic on the road in the morning. If we didn't get away soon we could get stuck in a traffic jam. Granddad didn't know. He took his time and dawdled to the car. The slower he went the more pressure I felt. We needed to rush. He finally slipped into the passenger seat and waited for me to set off. I angrily commanded him to fasten his safety belt. In shock he tugged at the belt and frantically rocked the buckle. It refused to click into place. We were wasting time. I had to do it for him so grabbed it and pushed. It didn't catch. In despair I stared down. A pound coin had fallen into the groove. I raked it out with the car key then it fastened. When it clicked I breathed until I relaxed and finally started the car and drove slowly down the drive.

Like a back seat driver Granddad commented on everything he saw. I found it unnecessary and without being rude said, "Granddad I expect you to observe the scenery and enjoy the ride. You don't need to tell me about the car in front or behind, I can see them too".

He stopped back seat driving, instead of looking out of the window he told me he had a dream. It made me think he was lucky to get some sleep, I didn't. If he could drive I would let him, and I would have happily fallen asleep in the passenger seat. I had to be pleasant and asked, "Did you? What about?"

"I dreamed about the MRF. People were sorting stuff out and putting it into piles".

I grinned. Driving and listening to him kept me awake. I yawned and asked, "Were they?"

He laughed then explained, "Someone was shovelling cans on to a wagon and they kept falling off".

I laughed at the thought of it. Only in dreams could someone shovel cans. In real life it can't be done and we agreed the only way would be to throw them. It made me wonder how recycled cans are loaded onto wagons. How does the MRF do it?

Over a short stretch of rough road the car shook and I told Granddad I visualised a pile of cans jumping and rolling on the back of a wagon going to the can factory. It was fun to imagine but we thought there must be a better way to transport recycled cans.

I knew the general direction to drive to the MRF but we didn't really know the way. We needed some help. Granddad found the route on Google and happily read out the on screen directions. When the building came into view we cheered and within a few minutes stopped near the entrance. The site stretched as far as we could see. Buildings spread out so far it could have been a small city. Stunned, I panicked and gasped "Look how tall it is". Granddad loves height but I don't. Those buildings looked too high for me. Touring the plant, climbing the buildings and walking from one end to the other would be a nerve racking experience. It would take all day and I needed to compose myself and relax.

"Breath!" Granddad advised and waited until I had courage to get out of the car. Immediately he said, "Don't worry, have a bar of chocolate and follow me". We marched to the gatehouse. The Security Guard stopped us, took our details and said we would have to go through the usual formalities.

"Formalities?" Granddad asked, "Do you mean red tape?"

With a wry smile the Guard nodded and explained "It usually takes half an hour. It's a Safety Induction to let you know the dangers and what to do if there is an emergency".

"Really?" Granddad said, "Don't we just run?"

The guard laughed, admitted he would run, but insisted the procedures have to be followed. He explained the Safety Induction would give us advice when to run and where to run, that sort of thing.

The virtual lecture took exactly half and hour. When it finished Granddad commented "That was the longest thirty minutes of my life". The Guard's expression gave the impression he had heard that a hundred times. He gave us safety clothing and identity badges to hang round our necks. He also assured us Joe would arrive soon.

Joe, a tall stout man arrived, introduced himself, said he would be our guide and took us outside. My blue bin stuff is always clean, so doesn't smell. I imagined everything would be clean and odour free, but I was wrong. Joe waved vaguely in the air, apologised for the smell and set off to a place he called the Hall.

Lifting his skull and cross bones pirate mask a little higher and obviously smirking Granddad pointed and asked, "Who do we look like?"

I quickly responded, "With your workman boots, yellow jacket, hat and big rubber gloves you look like a bandit bin man and I look like a yellow duck".

"A lot of ducks work here" Joe said, "you'll fit right in".

As we walked towards the plant the smell grew stronger. We were on our way to the source of the pong.

Granddad joked, "Let's get down and dirty!"

Joe didn't complain about the smell again, but the fact that some people put the wrong stuff in the blue bin narked him. He grumbled, "Some people think anything can recycled but it can't. We have to sort it, pick out the rubbish and chuck it away. This should be a clean job but my lads have to put up with this stink. Someone should tell people how to wash recyclables properly".

My face glowed with pride knowing I wash mine.

Granddad, an experienced, expert Bin Man had smelled lots of rotten stuff, some worse than others. He recognised something he really hated, held his nose and shouted, "I hate that smell. That is not recycling, it is food that has gone off! Mouldy cheese and cabbage!"

Joe agreed and was pleased to say in a year or two the Council will send food waste to another place for treatment in a bio-digester thing and he hoped people will put it in the bin provided and then the smell will not be so bad. With his experience he reckoned some people can't tell the difference between baby bottles and nappies, cardboard and toast. He took a deep breath and coughed, "We've had everything and we're trying to save the Planet. You asked to see it, but you wont like it!"

At least a kilometre long, the Hall had a conveyor down the middle stretching from one end of the building to the other. The conveyor motor roared and the belt, covered with waste, rattled. We didn't like the din and Joe shrugged and tutted,"It is a horrible job".

It was fascinating watching the conveyor and curiously amusing listening to Joe, tut, all the time. There was nothing we could do to improve the situation, we were there to learn. I said, "So this how it is done! The stuff out of the blue bins goes on the conveyor and your guys pick out the rubbish and I assume it is thrown away".

"Burned!" Joe said roughly. "And those guys are Pickers".

Joe meant I should show respect, use the professional title, they are called Pickers. He also made me realise stuff, like broken window glass, that I put in the blue bin because it looked recyclable, must have been picked out and burned. Joe had complained about how much work the Pickers have to do and I wondered if I should apologise for my mistakes. After careful consideration I decided my honest admission would not be appreciated and said nothing.

Joe coughed "This is where the process starts. If it can't be recycled my guys reject, or should I say eject the rubbish. They pick it out, throw it in the big bins beside the conveyor and at the end of the day send it to the incinerator". Troubled that so much rubbish is mixed with the recycled stuff Joe groaned, "In an ideal world people would be careful what they put in their blue bin and my team would have nothing to do. As you can see they are very busy all the time".

It was clear he thought picking should be a clean, not very busy job. He wanted to know we agreed. I did, and mentally apologised to the Pickers, accepted it was a one-off and vowed I wont do it again.

Granddad had a different opinion. He had spent years emptying smelly bins and driving to the Dump. He used to say it was an awful place where the wind blew dust like snow in a storm, and smelled of rotting rubbish. He had got used to it and didn't mind most smells or hard work. He casually remarked, "It is a job!"

Joe looked upset but ignored the comment, praised his team for doing a horrible job really well and talked about the next stage. The stage where stuff is sorted mechanically.

Granddad questioned, "What do you mean next stage? I thought the Pickers did everything!"

Joe calmly explained in the next stage machines separate everything into piles of glass, plastic, cardboard, aluminium and steel. He promised, "You will see everything on the tour".

We were close enough to the conveyor to see the Pickers at work, but Granddad wanted to do the job. He had a quick chat with Joe, asked the Lead Picker if he could help and began picking. Recycling waste rumbled and bumped along the conveyor belt quickly, so fast that he missed some bits and chased them with a defiant stare, daring them to jump off the belt themselves. Concerned he would scramble onto the belt to pick those pieces I warned him to keep his feet on the ground or he would be whisked away and sorted.

He heeded my warning and pointed out those offending pieces to the others, further along the line, so they could pick them.

Each Picker had a huge waste bin and seemed to be in competition with the others, working hard, to fill it as quickly as possible. Granddad enjoyed competing. He and the Lead Picker were winning and having so much fun that when the bin was full and Joe wanted to inspect the stuff they had rejected they didn't want to stop. Joe shouted very loud.

With a mixture of satisfaction and disgust Granddad showed him some black bin bags, non stick frying pans, bicycle chains, broken glass, pieces of pottery, an unfinished painting of a vase and the vase and lots of cardboard marked with soup and gravy. He held each item at arms length and, with turned up nose, commented, "This can't be recycled". Holding up the bicycle chain he remarked "Someone has lost this. They wont be going for a ride tonight". He threw it back in the bin and held up one of the other items. When he had shown the last item he asked, "Why do people put this rubbish in the blue bin? Don't they have a khaki one?"

His comment amused me and behind my mask I grinned, but at the same time thought some people are so silly, they must know they can't recycle frying pans. Joe looked in the bin, he was not amused, he complained it was unnecessary work for his Pickers.

"Those people make sorting difficult!" he protested. "Clean, sorted waste with no rubbish is valuable. It would be worthless if my team didn't clean it!"

Obviously exasperated he wanted to blame someone for the contamination. He confessed, "I don't know who to blame! I've not been able to work out who the offenders are or why they do what they do?" His hands clenched into fists and he said, "I'd give them a clip if I caught them".

People say all sorts of things when they feel mad. I thought there must be a better way and so did Granddad.

Joe continued to grumble then changed his mind, he wouldn't clip anyone but he would try to teach them what can be recycled. He said, "They have the bins, they just don't know how to use them. A khaki bin is for the rubbish and a blue one is for the future. People get confused, mixed up, or are they colour blind or…" He stopped trying to excuse them and blamed them for making his Pickers work so hard and called them awkward. He stopped again, looked at Granddad for inspiration, then exclaimed, "They all have a khaki bin! Why can't they use it?" His hands opened as he admitted defeat. He had vented his feelings and stopped being mad and said, "I give up!"

Joe had not thought when one bin is full people put their rubbish in any colour bin, even blue or green. Granddad had worked it out. He waited a moment then meekly suggested, "Maybe the khaki bin is full!"

Joe howled crossly "What?"

His response and the way Granddad said kacky, instead of khaki, made me laugh. Fortunately no one could see my face behind my mask. To add to Joe's woes Granddad also decided to tell him a few bits of rubbish had escaped his diligent Pickers and gone on to the next stage. There is never a good time to give bad news but Granddad wanted to know what happens to it?

Still grinning behind my mask I warned myself to be prepared. I expected Joe to blow-up. The more I thought about it the funnier it seemed, so to ensure no one could see my face I turned my back on them and looked at the gatehouse.

"A few!" Joe cried bitterly. "They'll have missed more than a few. Those bits will get mixed up with everything and go up there!"

He pointed into the distance. At the far end of the Hall the belt rose to another level, and resembling a fun fair ghost train, disappeared into a cave. Joe shouted, "That is the next stage!"

Granddad raised his hand to ask a question?

Joe stopped pointing. He realised Granddad had a question and before he asked it Joe complained the cold and noise made conversation difficult so he would take us for a cup of tea and a chat in the cabin.

CHAPTER 5

The cabin was a small workaday hut, not far from the Hall. I had the impression someone had rushed in and out again. They had left it untidy but I was grateful it provided shelter from the wind and noise. We took off our masks and Joe charged over to the sink in the corner to wash his hands. He didn't wait for the hot water to run through, he muttered Happy Birthday while he washed them in the freezing cold water. Granddad washed his next. Waiting for my turn I chose one of the two tables in the room and put three of the randomly scattered chairs in place for Granddad, Joe and me then looked round. Near the sink I noticed a cupboard and on top of it an electric kettle and a box of tea bags, bag of sugar, a tiny tin of sweeteners and a drum of powdered milk, all the things needed to make a brew. Joe switched on the kettle, took three well used cups from the cupboard and made the tea.

Protected from the breeze and just a trickle of air blowing through the open window, I soon felt warmer and would have asked Joe things like who buys recycled waste and why? Does recycling really help to stop the World getting too hot? But Granddad spoke first. "Picking is a warm job. Does the plant keep going day and night?"

Joe happily told him it never rests, there is never a day off, not even Christmas Day or New Year's Day. He smiled, "People keep making waste and we keep sorting it". He paused, waiting for us to laugh. Regrettably we didn't, and he didn't attempt to be funny again.

He groaned, "Christmas is probably our busiest time".

Granddad gabbled, "Christmas, cards, presents".

Joe advised, "Wrapping paper".

Granddad interrupted, "Used to burn it on the fire. Everyone burned wrapping paper and all sorts of rubbish, to keep warm. Smelly and smoky but we were cold and had to keep warm so burned anything. We don't have open fires any more. The smoke made smog and smog killed people so we stopped using open fires and got central heating".

I said to myself, I didn't like the coal fire. I was about ten when we got central heating. Joe said he had never burned anything on an open fire and only seen one in a museum. I assumed he was younger than he looked.

He couldn't wait to tell his Christmas story. "Last Christmas a lot of fancy wrapping paper came in. The Hall floor was covered with it. People know we send newspapers and office paper to be recycled, but don't realise we don't take shiny Christmas wrapping paper. It can't be recycled because it is covered in a thin film of plastic or covered with sticky tape and glitter. It is rubbish!"

Trying not to sound sarcastic I said, "A happy Christmas story Joe. Thank you for telling me. I think I put mine in the blue bin instead of the khaki one, sorry".

Joe looked smug, he said, "I don't suppose you did it on purpose. Anyone can make a mistake and you are allowed one mistake at Christmas, so I'll let you off".

His tone made me feel told-off, not forgiven, but I acted grateful, said thank you, and for no particular reason, just to make conversation, I asked, "Why cover the floor?"

He rushed to tell me. "We didn't do it deliberately. It just seemed to happen. The bins filled up and overflowed with paper. The teams liked the Christmas look and had a competition to see who got the best decorated floor? It might seem odd," he added, "but it helped us to be cheerful at Christmas".

Joe finished his story and his tea and insisted we should go back to the Hall. There was no time to ask my questions. I thought I would ask on the way back to the Hall but Joe talked about his Pickers, the scrap and rubbish and how the recycling flows along the conveyor, up a level to the next stage.

"I will show you" he assured us. When we walked into the Hall he pointed to a set of metal stairs at the far end, almost a kilometre away and said, "Up there!" He walked towards them. I followed him and Granddad followed me.

Walking along side the conveyor belt, playing games, Granddad had a friendly competition with the Pickers. It was amusing watching him try to steal bits and pieces of rubbish from the belt and see the Pickers rush to grab them before he did. Each time he was beaten he turned and shrugged his shoulders, as if he didn't care, but tried again and again. Half way along the Hall I noticed we were leaving him behind so shouted, "Come on Granddad! Run!" He sprinted, caught up, stopped messing about and behaved. The stairs were incredibly steep. Trudging up them, watching the recycling rattle alongside made me wish the conveyor was an escalator. I would have appreciated a moving stair case to take me from the bottom to the top, to the next level. Unfortunately it was conveying recycling waste from the ground floor to the next one. There was no room for me, I had to climb. Every step clanged, the recycling rattled and the noise in the Hall echoed creating a really uncomfortable atmosphere.

At the top, on the gallery, holding the hand-rail tightly, panting, struggling for breath I thanked heaven I had made it. Weary, wobbly and unintentionally looking down into the Hall my mind played tricks. I stood still yet everything around me moved. Feeling dizzy I grabbed on to the hand rail to reassure myself the world was not in motion. It gave me confidence to stare into the distance. The Hall seemed vast, the conveyor strange and the Pickers unreal. I could actually see waste being tipped on to the conveyor, the beginning of its journey, and the Pickers flitting from one place to another, like butterflies, stripping out the rubbish. Comically, as the conveyor moved the waste made faces, some happy, enjoying the ride, some sad, uncomfortable at being jiggled about, and some very worried about what might happen when they reach the next stage. On the upward slope to the cave, some shuffled down, as if they sensed danger, but the belt kept pulling them until, with a quiet gasp, they entered the cave and disappeared.

Joe and I, puffing like old men, were amazed to see Granddad almost float up the stairs. On the gallery he did a pirouette, pointed to the cave and shouted, "What happens in there?"

Conserving his energy and breath Joe briefly gasped, "Go in".

Granddad ushered me to go in first. I knew it would scare me but I squeezed through the little doorway, experienced the noise and shaking platform and quickly jumped out again.

"I'll go!" Granddad shouted, and like a Commando on a mission, made his way through the doorway. I watched him move to his left, towards the cave entrance then follow the belt. At shoulder height it rumbled along behind a clear glass shield, then dipped down. He followed it slowly, knelt down and scrambled along on his hands and knees until he unexpectedly bumped his hat on an invisible wall of glass, and yelled. I would never forget that scream and felt sure I would see that scene many times in my dreams. Shocked, but otherwise unharmed, he soon recovered and began pointing, waving his arms and shouting. "It's like a fair ground ride!"

Drawing pictures in the air he described the movement of the belt. "It loops down, along and then ends. Everything falls down onto a wheel!"

I shouted, "Wheel?" With my hand stirring round I shouted, "Do you mean like a round-a-bout?"

He spread his arms as far apart as he could and shouted "Wide! Tins stick to it and are scraped off. They fall down a tube! It's fun! Why don't you take a look?"

Shaking my head furiously I complained "Not brave enough. It is too small and claustrophobic for me. I don't like the noise!"

Granddad shook his head and I could sense he meant if he could do it so could I, but I couldn't.

I understood the tins stick to the wheel so shouted "It must be magnetic! Steel tins stick to magnets. The magnet collects tins!" I realised the other stuff must go somewhere so I shouted "Where does the other stuff go?"

His hand demonstrated something flying then dropping straight down. He shouted, "It falls over the edge and lands on another conveyor belt". He continued, "That belt takes it to a place where red cans bounce or jump out". This time both his hands set off on a flight together until they separated, one flew up and the other down. I assumed the one going up must be a can and the ones going down, everything else.

Joe had got his breath back and informed me there is a magnet that catches the steel tins and a different kind of magnet that separates the aluminium cans. Granddad, couldn't hear Joe's explanation and kept demonstrating with his hands how cans jump.

It looked fun, I had to see, so took a deep breath and stepped inside the cave. Following the belt, the way Granddad did, but more cautiously so I didn't bang my head,

I saw what he meant about sticking and jumping. Amazed, and entertained by the sticky wheel and jumping cans I forgot my fear and laughed. Stepping on to the gallery again with my hands in the air I told Granddad I had never seen anything like it and wanted Joe to explain.

Joe wanted to know if we knew about bar magnets. "Everyone knows about magnets" Granddad scoffed. "I learned at school bar magnets have North at one end and South at the other".

Behind his mask Joe grinned. "The North end of one magnet sticks to the South end of another but the North end jumps away from another North end and… You know what I mean?"

Granddad and I nodded so Joe carried on. "The wheel is called a rolling roller and it is magnetic. When you've seen it one or two hundred times and you know how it works it isn't quite so incredible. You know tins are made of steel and steel sticks to magnets".

Granddad nudged me and reminded me I had shown him how a fridge magnet stuck to the beans tin. It was hard to hear what Joe said but I wanted to hear and listened carefully. He said, "The rolling roller is magnetic and tins stick to it. As they go round they are scraped off and drop down the tin tube".

I gasped, "Fascinating! Whoever thought of that?"

"Don't know" Joe shrugged, "but it works for tins".

He had confidently told us why tins stick to magnets but found it harder to explain why aluminium cans jump. When he finished explaining I was not sure I understood so asked him to say it again. He shouted, "Under the belt there is a thing, he said I'll call it Eddy. When Eddy is switched on it becomes a giant magnet. When aluminium cans go over it they become magnets and like North jumps way from North, they jump off the belt. They go down the aluminium tube and land in a pile at the bottom. Clever isn't it?"

Joe's explanation made it sound simple. Switch on and let Eddy do the rest. Granddad knew all about bar magnets. He didn't know anything about Eddy and wanted more information. Joe only knew Eddy is an electro magnet and it makes cans jump. To save embarrassment he rounded off saying, "All the tins and cans that come into the cave either stick or jump".

We had assumed stuff would be separated at the MRF and someone would buy a pile of it and shovel it into a wagon. Granddad said to Joe, "Then you sell a pile of tins or cans or whatever!"

"More to it than that!" Joe responded. "They have to be squashed! We don't sell piles, we sell cubes". I noticed the enthusiasm in his voice when he said squashed and thought that must be his favourite part of the job. His enthusiasm continued, he said, "When there are enough, we squash them into cubes. Each cube weighs a tonne. That is one thousand kilograms". It is quite hard to sound smug and arrogant when you shout but Joe smiled under his mask then with obvious satisfaction said, "That is a million grams, you know".

I did know but chose not to tell him. He went on to tell us the cube is called a bale and each one is stored in the warehouse until someone buys it.

"A bale?" Granddad asked.

I asked, "Who buys them?"

Joe answered, "You will see a bale before you go. Anyone, can buy one".

Everything we had seen and done, the Hall, conveyor belt, rolling roller and Eddy the electromagnet had been fascinating. I looked forward to seeing how plastic, glass and cardboard are separated. Would there be more Pickers at the other side of the plant or some incredible new machine? I couldn't wait to find out.

CHAPTER 6

Tired of shouting Joe motioned a cup of tea and walked towards the stairs. “Hold on to the rails!” he commanded. “It’s a long way down if you fall!”

He didn’t have to tell me, I had walked up and knew. Holding the hand-rail tightly and stepping slowly I make a point of not looking too far ahead, in case it made me feel dizzy.

When we reached the ground Joe and I walked steadily but Granddad had lots of energy. Pretending to steal the rubbish from the belt he played games with the Pickers, again. Joe and I followed him, talked about scrap, tins, cans and rubbish and laughed at Granddad’s antics.

The excitement, the noise, the cold, nervousness descending the stairs and trudging through the Hall wore me out. In the quiet of the cabin my ears were ringing and my hands trembled, I was cold. Granddad skipped and jumped all the way and had something important on his mind. Away from the plant, we didn’t have to shout, but he did. “What’s next?”

Joe almost whispered, “Good question. Do you want to see the next stage?”

Granddad nodded insanely. I agreed and joined in, “Yes we do”.

Joe didn’t answer immediately, he gazed across the room and seemed to be thinking until finally he told us we can’t.

Granddad complained “That’s annoying!”

Joe put his hands in the air, as if in surrender, and said he couldn’t do anything.

Granddad argued, "We came to see what you do with the recycled stuff? To see how the place works. We haven't seen the cardboard, glass and plastic. Is it a secret?"

Startled, Joe replied, "Oh no! It's not a secret. You just can't see it. They are sorted down a tunnel. You can't see inside. I can tell you how it works".

"Go on then!" Granddad insisted.

Joe's eyes suggested he wished he hadn't volunteered to tell us, but knew he had too. "They are spotted by a RED EYE SEPARATOR. It pushes them this way and that. They go down tubes and end up in piles. You can see the tunnel but not what goes on inside".

"Red Eye Separator" Granddad said. Then with lots of enthusiasm, "The latest up to date all singing, all dancing piece of equipment. Stuff must go through that tunnel so fast it wont have time to blink and it must have a million hands".

"I don't think so" Joe said cautiously, "it doesn't have any hands, it puffs".

"I would think it does" Granddad joked, "the rate it works it must be puffed out".

Exasperated, Joe explained, "Inside the tunnel there is a lane for cardboard, one for glass and another for plastic. All Red Eye has to do is blow everything into the right lane".

Hoping Joe would change his mind Granddad put on his miserable, disappointed face and asked to see inside the tunnel. Joe shook his head, held up his hands and told him that if he really wanted to see he would have to go down the tunnel and end up heavens knows where.

Granddad grumbled, "How boring. I wanted to see it all. Is that the end of the tour?"

"Look!" Joe said. "Have you enjoyed the tour so far?"

Still looking depressed Granddad told him he had. He then seemed to remember we were supposed to be experts and told Joe he had only been joking. We knew about the tunnel and it would be difficult to see old Red Eye. He claimed he hoped Joe's Facility had found a new way to separate stuff.

Joe mocked, "You are the expert, you tell me. I hoped you experts would have a new way. We haven't".

Touché, I thought, you tried to fool Joe but he has the answers.

He had been told it is impossible to see inside the tunnel but Granddad continued to play act. He looked really sad, sniffed and sulked for a minute or two. His miserableness did not get him the sympathy he hoped for so he tried a different approach. He thanked Joe for letting him work with the Pickers and showing him Eddy and the magnets and told him he understood it was not his fault. He was clearly attention seeking. His antics amused me but troubled Joe and when he asked if Joe would mind taking us to see what happens to the stuff that falls down the tubes, Joe agreed. "Be a pleasure! I'll take you to the DROP-IN point where the bins are filled. You can see stuff being squashed into bales and put on the shelves. Come on!"

Granddad chatted all the way so Joe knew all about him and the University he went to, the number of years he has been an expert and how much he was looking forward to seeing cans being squashed. I knew Granddad had looked disappointed because he thought he wasn't going to get his own way. I also knew he made it all up. He had never been to University and never been an expert, however, Joe listened. When we reached the drop-in point Granddad stopped talking and Joe acted as tour guide. "Tins drop out of the tin tube and into that enormous bin and the aluminium ones drop into that one".

With his happy face on, Granddad watched tins drop out of the tin tube, land noisily at the top of the pile and jump high in the air. Tumbling down the hill of tins they performed summersaults, flips and cartwheels until they found a place to stop and settle. They only moved again when other tins bounced on them.

The tin tub filled quickly and before it over flowed a high speed forklift truck lifted it out of the way and replaced it with an empty one.

Joe gave a commentary "The bin is full… that one is empty… the truck driver moves the full one and puts the empty in its place. Speedy the fork lift truck driver will take the full bin to Bosh, the Baler".

He had run out of things to say about the process and looked uneasy. He couldn't just stand and watch so he told us "The fork lift truck driver is called Speedy because he has a reputation for rushing".

Watching the truck race round the yard, lifting bins and putting them down I wondered if I should ask if Speedy has a proper name. Before asking I decided Joe might not know it and that would be embarrassing. It would be sensible to let him do the talking and tell us whatever he wanted.

Unable to stay quiet for long Joe then said, "He speeds everywhere. That's why we call him Speedy".

The truck raced backwards and forwards and the bin full of tins was taken to a big black box. Joe gave his commentary. "Speedy is taking that bin to Bosh. The tins will be compressed and come out in a big block".

The activity at the drop-in point was noisy but entertaining, however there was more to see. Joe shouted "Come to the Power House. We can watch Bosh squash the tins from there. Don't rush".

Granddad didn't like the idea of not rushing, he wanted to get there and it annoyed him that Joe and I didn't rush, we took our time.

Concerned we might not appreciate Bosh is the baler Joe pointed out that it looks like a strong box, but it isn't. He hadn't really smiled a lot during the visit, but he smiled and positively exuded pleasure when he said, "Those tins are about to be squashed. You'll see, they will be flat as pancakes when the job is finished, squashed together in a giant cube".

Speedy whizzed across the yard and Granddad asked, "Can I have a go?"

I gasped, he couldn't ride a bike without wobbling and had never driven a truck. He would certainly crash and we would have to run or get run cover. I thought if Joe gives him permission I'll look for protection, somewhere safe to hide.

Joe hesitated before answering. That gave me time to consider my options. I smiled, thinking it would be fun to watch, and I would be quite safe if I hid behind the big black boxes. They looked sturdy enough to protect me if he accidentally drove into one and I would enjoy the spectacle.

Joe found a sort of in between option that pleased me because we would all be safe, but disappointed me because I'd miss the performance and Granddad might sulk. "Speedy might give you a lift on his truck, but I don't think he'll let you drive".

With a frown Granddad said he'd never driven a truck and didn't want to drive one, he wanted to squash the tins.

Coughing into his mask Joe asked, "Have you got a Baler Button Pusher license?"

Granddad protested. "You cannot be serious! I don't need a Baler Button Pusher license to push a button!"

Joe grinned, he had his sense of humour back. "Just joking! You don't need one, but you will have to listen to ARCHIE. Archie will tell you when to push".

I wondered if that was another joke so asked "Who is Archie?"

Without a smile Joe told Granddad Archie is an artificially intelligent android, who lives in the Power House.

It sounded incredible that an android should have to give Granddad permission to press a button. It had to be a joke. I asked him to tell me more about Archie. With a condescending tone he advised me Archie is a clever, artificial intelligent machine. Not a real person!

Blushing, feeling foolish and too embarrassed to tell him it was a joke, I thanked him for his helpful information and waited to be told why Archie has the responsibility, and not a person like Speedy. Joe didn't wait long, he said, "It would be a tragedy if someone got squashed. Archie is wired to Bosh and can tell if it is empty or full and can detect body heat, movement and breathing and if there is someone inside, Archie will know. It also detects if the door is shut and locked properly and only gives the order to push the button when it is safe. Real people make mistakes but Archie never does".

The information seemed interesting I just found it hard to concentrate and my eyes must have shown it. Joe commented "I know Archie sounds boring but it doesn't only tell when the operation is finished and the door unlocked, it celebrates!"

I was beginning to think Archie really is a fun android.

Speedy waved from the Powerhouse and sounding like a commentator Joe said, "Speedy is almost ready to push the button. You can do the next one. Come on, if you want to watch we will have to go inside".

An android voice announced, "Push the button," Speedy obeyed. A motor whined and tins rattled. The squashing had begun. In the final moments the motor whined louder as it could not squash the tins any flatter. It stopped then reversed ready for the next batch of tins. Archie called "Process complete! Let's celebrate!"

The situation felt surreal, machines don't have feelings. In a voice that reminded me of a washing machine announcing the wash cycle has finished Archie wanted us to celebrate. This machine said, "Celebrate. The door is unlocked" and I imagined it virtually raised a glass. I wanted to join in the celebration.

Speedy ran, opened the door, then taking great care not to hit anything, drove his truck forks under the newly formed bale. He expertly lifted it and slowly reversed out, lowered it, stopped his truck engine and rushed inside the baler with a sweeping brush. He swept several tins, that had fallen onto the floor and escaped being crushed, into a bin bag, then mounted his truck. I watched him steadily lift the bale then race into the distance and disappear.

In the Power House Granddad inspected the control panel buttons, nobs and switches then said to Joe "I like Archie. You'll have to introduce me".

Joe responded, "Sure, be my pleasure, I'll introduce you". He pointed to rows of buttons and told Granddad, "One for each baler".

"Each baler?" Granddad queried. "Why do you have more than one?"

Joe loved to explain things and show his knowledge. Vaguely pointing accusingly at the row of balers he explained, "Speedy swept out some tins. If he missed any they would have mixed in the next bale. If the next one is plastic there will be tins in plastic. This is a Material

Recovery Facility. Stuff arrives here all mixed up together and nobody wants it. Tins are made of steel. Steel is worth a lot of money. I separate it, someone buys it to make something. They don't want tins in plastic, do they?"

Granddad listened intently to Joe's messages, separate recyclables, do not mix them and someone will buy them. He had always told me, where there's muck there's money, and I thought the idea of making money selling bales of recyclables appealed to him. He said, "No good mixing them again is it Joe?"

Truck lights flashed through the Power House window. Speedy arrived with a bin full of aluminium cans, put it down and opened a baler door. A button on the control panel lit up. Joe pointed to it and told Granddad that was the one he would have to push. Speedy opened the baler door, checked inside, placed the bin inside and closed and locked the door. He waved to let Joe know the system was set, ready to go, and ran into the Power House. Archie took a minute or two to do the checks then announced, "Baler is ready. Push the button!"

Granddad's finger hovered above the button, but could not push it. Joe had seen that moment of indecision many times, people uncertain whether to obey Archie or wait. He diagnosed, "Beginners nerves! He wont be able to do it until I tell him". He waved and nodded and Granddad gleefully pressed the button. The motor whined and although the windows dulled the noise we heard the lamentable sound of thousands of cans shuffling to avoid being pressed. When they couldn't shuffle any more, they folded, crumpled and cracked. Finally the crushing stopped, the motor ran in reverse and in the peculiar, washing machine voice, Archie announced "The door is unlocked".

I imitated Archie's mechanical voice and shouted, "The cycle has finished" but had forgotten Archie would say, "Well done! Let's celebrate!" and laughed when I heard it.

We raised our imaginary glasses, knocked them together to salute Granddad's success and pretended to celebrate.

Speedy rushed to open the baler door, hauled out the massive, perfectly formed metal cube and gave the thumbs up. Unexpectedly feeling proud that my Granddad had made a bale of aluminium cans, I slapped his back. Joe shook his hand and congratulated him. "Granddad, you have successfully squashed a tonne of cans and made that bale. You deserve a prize. What would you like?"

Trembling with excitement and embarrassment Granddad could hardly speak. Finally, modestly he said, "I don't. That baler does. It has squashed all those cans". He seemed to think, then asked, " What did you say it is called?"

"Its name?" Joe said quietly. "I call it..." He stopped then thoughtfully told Granddad "I call it a naff name. You can give it any name you like".

Granddad gazed at it through the Power House window, shook his head slowly and muttered he wanted to give it a name that shows respect. Joe put his arm affectionately round his shoulders and tried to encourage him. "Come on Granddad you can give it one. What are you going to call it?"

As if in a trance Granddad uttered "The Black Box".

Joe repeated it. "The Black Box! That is a great name for a baler!"

We pretended to raise our glasses and toasted, "The Black Box!"

With his arm still round his shoulder, Joe asked "Would you like to see what happens next?"

Granddad woke from his trance and replied, "Yes please!"

Joe pointed to a building in the distance and told us it is the warehouse where bales are stored. He said, "Bales are placed on shelves for buyers to view, and whoever buys them takes them away. I'll show you".

Before we set off he advised, "Walk on the path. There are a few fork lift trucks flying about. Speedy is not the only one. But he is the fastest".

We took our time and sauntered slowly past Speedy. He shouted and waved a bunch of papers Joe recognised and commented, "Registration documents. Those forms take ages to fill in so we can take our time".

Walking single file, following Joe, I chuckled thinking we had overtaken the fastest truck driver on the plant, however Granddad panicked. He couldn't believe Speedy would be held up for ages. He wanted to go faster, be at the warehouse and confident he would see his bale lifted and put on its shelf. We were still chatting and plodding in single file when Speedy raced by. Joe assured us he would have to show his bale paperwork, have it stamped and other formalities so there was no need to worry. We would get there before him.

Granddad, was not convinced, he impatiently slid in front of me, then Joe and trotted ahead.

"Wait!" Joe shouted, but Granddad didn't listen. He ran, turned a corner and disappeared.

Putting on his tour guide head Joe informed me Granddad must have got to the warehouse. "There are hundreds of aisles with shelves, mezzanine floors, steel partitions and pallet racking in there" and with a sense of urgency advised, "He wont know where Speedy has gone. He's sure to get lost. We'd better hurry".

Granddad arrived at the warehouse and gasped. The building was as big as an aircraft hanger, bigger than the Hall and very quiet. He wanted to ask for directions so shouted, "Hello". No one replied. His echo returned a few seconds later and he knew he was alone. This is big, he told himself, and there is no one here. There were rows and rows of shelves. He wondered where Speedy would put his bale and decided to look. He ran round the building up one aisle and down another searching for the aluminium shelf. He was still running when Joe and I arrived. We heard him panting. I called, "Granddad!" and he ran to meet us.

Gasping for breath Granddad told us he had looked everywhere for the aluminium aisle, but couldn't find it.

"Could be in the wrong warehouse" Joe joked, "Did you notice the other one. It is bigger than this".

Granddad's eyes opened wide in disbelief. He gasped, "No!"

I said, "Very funny. It is OK, Granddad, there isn't another warehouse".

Joe laughed, "You are a rebel Granddad, you should do as you are told. Speedy is on his way. I can hear him. He wont be long".

Roaring into the building, Speedy tooted swung to his right and raced along until he turned into one of the aisles and disappeared. He knew we wanted to watch him ceremoniously lift Granddad's bale into place and we expected him to wait, however, we heard him rev loudly. We had the impression he had started without us.

With a sense of urgency Joe shouted, "Come on! We had better rush. He wont hang about!" We followed the noise and ran. Turning into the aisle we saw the bale still on the floor, Speedy revved furiously and beneath his mask grinned broadly. He had tricked us. Pretending not to care Joe gave him the thumbs up. Speedy continued to tease us and lifted the bale very slowly up to the shelf and very gently put it in place. We cheered, but Speedy had not finished. He unfurled a huge banner and stuck it on the bale. In big letters it said, GRANDDAD'S BALE.

This really was the end of the tour. We had seen sorting from beginning to end and had lots of wonderful memories. Steel tins sticking to a magnet, aluminium cans jumping in the Eddy Current, Granddad picking rubbish but best of all he pushed the button and his block was on a shelf in the warehouse. We clapped and cheered, "Well done, Granddad".

He didn't care for the appreciation, but enjoyed the visit and didn't want it to end. He turned to Joe and asked, "What next?"

With a hand gesture that seemed to mean anything Joe said, "Anyone can buy it". Then joked, "Do you want it? It would be a great souvenir and I'll do you a special price".

Granddad stopped himself saying he didn't want a heap of scrap. Instead he asked what he would do with it?

I would have told him he could make cars, planes, frames, phones, fridges, televisions, computers, electric kettles, the list seemed endless but Joe said, "Cans!"

Granddad did not want to hear that. He wanted to be told all the things I thought of. He looked up to the sky and moaned, "I know".

Joe suddenly appreciated he should highlight aluminium is much more useful than that and gave an excellent example of something made from it, window frames.

Granddad's windows were glass and the frames made of wood. He was about to let Joe know but I stopped him. I didn't want an argument at the end of our tour so interrupted him and confirmed, “They are! My window frames are made of aluminium”.

Although he didn’t really know, he took the hint and gave the impression he did. “Of course they are, silly me”.

Granddad understood we should be grateful and show our appreciation. He said thank you a million times and assured Joe he could see aluminium is extremely useful, but laughed at the idea of taking a cube home even if it would make a wonderful monument for the garden.

Granddad didn’t say much as we walked from the warehouse to the gatehouse until we were almost there. He observed, “No rubbish anywhere. The place is very clean, well done”. Joe appreciated the compliment. He pointed to a neighbouring plant and said, “Speedy takes all the rubbish to the Waste to Energy plant over there”.

Granddad looked curious. I hoped he wouldn’t ask Joe any more questions but could tell he was about to. In an attempt to stop him I said, “We are experts. We know that!”.

Granddad said, “That’s a fancy title. What does it mean?”

I’d forgotten how much Joe likes to give any information. Offhand he said, “They burn rubbish! They burn waste and make electricity. Very useful!”

Granddad whispered urgently, “Sounds fun Freddy. Can you arrange a visit. I want to see inside the Waste to Energy plant. Let’s have a look”.

I had been very lucky to arrange the MRF tour and did not expect to be able to have a look. MRF and Waste to Energy Plants are not holiday destinations, resorts, places people go for a day out. We would be unlikely to be given permission, though if we were, it would be amazing.

I didn’t want to say, no, so half-heartedly said, “Don’t think they’ll let us in”.

Granddad sounded upset and even his mask could not hide his sulky face and protruding bottom lip.

"Granddad!" I said, sharply in an attempt to stop him being childish and wanting his own way.

Joe felt sympathetic and didn't approve of my reprimand. He didn't want Granddad to be upset, he wanted to cheer him up and told him, "Can't have you being upset Granddad. I'll see what I can do".

Granddad pulled his pet lip where it should be and cheekily stuck his tongue out at me while we waited for Joe to make the phone call.

A minute later he gave us the news. Sammy would give us a quick tour of the Waste to Energy plant.

I thought it wont be quick, Granddad has an insatiable appetite for knowledge and will bombard Sammy with questions. Joe must have thought the same, he smiled such a big smile his face mask stretched so far across his face he complained it didn't fit and pulled it back into place. "Er hum!" he coughed, then cautioned, "Don't expect too much, Sammy is only new so don't ask too many questions".

Granddad didn't reply. I grinned and muttered, "OK, We wont let you down" but knew we might.

Joe had been more helpful than we could ever have hoped. I told him we had enjoyed the experience and learned a lot and we were now even more expert than we were before. He seemed to know we were not experts at all and sounded a bit sarcastic when he said, "We've had a few experts visit, but you are the best".

Granddad made a point of saying he had enjoyed himself and will keep in touch and asked for directions to the Waste to Energy plant?

Joe grinned, "Speedy will drop you off".

With a vision of Speedy racing along with Granddad and me sitting on the forks of his truck, I checked to see if Joe's mask slipped again. It didn't, so I was hopeful he had arranged some other, safer, form of transport.

CHAPTER 7

A shiny blue car stopped beside us. The driver wore a fancy dress chauffeur hat and uniform. We didn't recognise Speedy until he shouted, "Come on you two, we haven't got all day. I've got to take you to that place over there".

Sitting regally on the back seat Granddad said, "I've never been in one of these".

Sitting in the front, feeling the leather upholstery and seeing all the knobs and dials on the dash board I thought Speedy was going to say Rolls Royce. He began "It's one of those..." then seemed to have forgotten what he was going to say and ad libbed, "can't remember what it is".

"Car" Granddad said helpfully. "It's a car. I've never been in one like this".

Speedy tittered, and laughed even more when I told him it is true. "We drove down in my car and would go home in it if Granddad didn't get us into too much trouble. He has never been in a car like this and neither have I".

Speedy commented, "Neither have I, but I like it".

Granddad remarked, "Very quiet. I can only hear a bit of road noise. Can't hear the motor".

Speedy looked at Granddad through the rear view mirror and told him, "That's because the motor is electric. Electric motors are amazingly quiet, and it is very fast. Watch it go when I accelerate".

From my position in the front I could see his foot press the accelerator pedal right down to the floor and we seemed to fly. I checked my seat belt, and Granddad checked his and we both held on to anything we could hold on to as the car went faster. Thinking he had already pressed the accelerator down as far as possible, I coolly said, "Smooth ride" then asked, "What is the top speed?"

He pressed his foot down so hard the pedal stuck on the floor and he promised, "I'll find out". The blood emptied from my face and didn't return until he slowed down to drop us off at the Waste to Energy plant gatehouse.

Shakily opening the car door and putting my foot on the ground I joked, "Must do that again some time". Speedy did not reply, he rushed to open Granddad's door and ordered, "Call me when you've finished and I'll pick you up".

I did not enjoy that high speed, hair raising ride, Granddad did. While I trembled he grinned. Oddly he thought sound travels faster than light and excitedly congratulated Speedy for travelling fast as light and hoped to break the sound barrier next time. I laughed, "Light travels faster than sound, Granddad" and Speedy giggled, "I will try".

I thought, when Sammy finishes our tour of the Waste to Energy plant it would be pleasant to walk back to the MRF.

Granddad had other plans. He and Speedy, whispered together and arranged for Speedy to collect us. To please Granddad I agreed. He had his own way, as usual, and jumped and bounced with excitement.

Speedy sped off and laughed and shouted, "See you later Granddad!"

Granddad waved and shouted. "See you later!"

I snapped "Don't encourage him Granddad. I'm still shaking. I don't like high speed. I'm not a high speedster".

Granddad screamed "I am!" and carried on waving and shouting until the car turned and disappeared.

This was the Waste to Energy plant, the place the Council sends all the rubbish to be burned. The sign on the gate proudly boasted, WE TURN RUBBISH INTO ELECTRICITY.

Through the gatehouse window the guard smirked behind his mask. I didn't know what he had been told about us but probably formed his own opinion seeing Granddad jump up and down, shouting and making a spectacle of himself. I wanted to make the right impression, we had to be more composed in case Joe told him we are experts. "Granddad" I hissed, "Behave" and gave him a few minutes to settle down.

Waiting, I observed a succession of wagons full of smelly waste, arrived every few minutes. The guard booked them in and told them where to go then monitored them on a number of screens as they drove to a building directly ahead and unloaded. When the empty wagons drove back to the gatehouse he flagged them down, ticked them off his list and raised the barrier so they could leave the site. It seemed well organised, he recorded all arrivals and departures. I hoped he was expecting us. Walking to the gatehouse, looking past the barrier into the site I noticed no litter, no mess, the place looked remarkably clean. It seemed too clean. I read the sign and asked Granddad if we had come to the right place?

He read the sign and looked into the air. He expected to see choking black smoke pouring from the very tall chimney but it was not. The stuff billowing out of it looked like steam. He sniffed and replied, "I don't know. Better check in at the gatehouse".

The guard grinned and welcomed us, "Safe as houses in here. You can go on site when you've seen the Safety Induction video. Only takes half an hour".

He was right, he greeted us when we emerged from the small theatre, exactly thirty minutes later. He asked what we thought and Granddad was honest, he said, "Longest half hour of the day. I'm glad it's over". The guard grinned, "They all say that" and almost subconsciously looked at the telephone and said he had called Sammy.

Impatiently waiting for our guide we saw a guy in the distance, wearing red boots, pink face mask and wobbly yellow hat walking towards us. We both said, "Sammy!"

Half a century ago engineers wore black boots, blue overalls and a flat hat. Times have changed but Granddad hadn't and carelessly commented "Real engineers don't wear red boots".

Things have changed. Council Bin Men didn't used to wear Hi Vis jackets but they do now. Engineers wear anything they like. If it is comfortable, suits their personality and is safe no one complains as long as they do a good job. I felt sure everyone would agree people are not labelled or judged by what they wear. I whispered, "We should behave, not argue and not mention dress sense in case we offend Sammy".

Granddad muttered defiance, but his attitude changed completely when Sammy apologised for making us wait and offered to take us for lunch. We had not eaten for hours and I wondered if he behaved badly because he was hungry. On the way to the canteen he bombard Sammy with questions. I would have asked a few myself but they never stopped talking. I watched the wagons again. They all looked the same, could have come from anywhere and they were all taking waste to be burned to make electricity. I wondered how the plant makes electricity from rubbish, but had no chance of asking.

In the canteen Sammy had to see someone and very kindly suggested we should go on ahead and order our meals. Generally I'd have a sandwich for lunch but having walked round the MRF and been busier than usual I had an enormous appetite. Granddad must have had the same feeling. We both piled food on our plates and hurried to the table.

I resented being excluded from the conversation on the way to the canteen. I felt jealous that Granddad did all the talking. I wanted to know about the Waste to Energy plant so grudgingly said to him

"You two had a good chat. What do you know about this place?"

He looked pleased to tell me, "Nice chap. New, very polite, quiet voice, keeps fit, plays squash, that sort of thing".

He had asked personal questions and probably knew more about Sammy than he did about me! I didn't want to know about Sammy so shrugged, "Very nice".

He did not take the hint. He told me Sammy would normally go jogging at lunch time but was going to have something with us to be sociable. We were guests and no matter how hungry I felt I had to wait for my not very hungry host. I said, sarcastically "How nice, how thoughtful". I wanted to start eating immediately but smiled and lied, "I don't mind waiting".

Being busy, occupied, doing something, anything, helps to forget about hunger. With a plate of food in front of me my only option seemed to be to play with it. I picked up my fork and slowly shifted salad and chips from one side of the plate to the other. Sammy arrived and said, "The boss wanted to tell me Joe had phoned and I have to show you everything. It's a good thing I'm only having tea and biscuits. We will have to get started".

With a fork full of chips and salad, about to begin eating, I looked up and saw Sammy without the mask, hat and coat. My appetite disappeared and my face turn red with embarrassment. Granddad smirked "Didn't you know Sammy is a lady?"

CHAPTER 8

Granddad is a ladies-man, finds them easy to talk to, so it made sense he got on well with her, and she got on well with him. This tour was going to be Granddad's fun day out with Sammy and I would enjoy finding out how a Waste to Energy plant works. She chatted with him and I devoured one chip after another. A few minutes later she commented that I had been very quiet, and to include me in the conversation asked if I like to be called Freddy or have a middle name or nick name or something else?

With a mouth full of chips and salad I could only shake my head.

She took the hint. She said, "I am called Samantha but I like my friends to call me Sammy".

She had directed her comment to me but Granddad told her he liked the name Samantha and everyone calls him Granddad.

With a mouth full of food I chuckled. I called him Granddad, however, when he worked for the Council he went round emptying bins. He was very popular and most people call him the Bin Man.

Determined to make me say something, Sammy tilted her head sideways to attract my attention then focused on the top of my head. She asked, "Do you?"

It seemed obvious she knew how to make me talk. She would keep looking until I responded. "Yes," I stuttered, "I do like the name, it suits you".

"I like the name Freddy too. I will call you two Freddy and Granddad. How does that sound?"

Trying to sound enthusiastic I stuttered, "Very friendly".

She grinned, lowered her head, unwrapped her biscuit, and said, “What do you think about the MRF?”

Granddad answered “Fun! We saw everything”.

Trying again to include me in the conversation she looked into my eyes, moved her head sideways, and queried, “Did you?”

With a mouth full of food, unable to speak, and distracted by the wriggling curls in her long blonde hair, I didn’t answer. We had a look round for a few hours, not long enough to see everything. Hoping Granddad would tell her I nodded and pointed to him. She didn’t take her eyes off me until I managed to say, “Granddad can tell you all about it. Can’t you Granddad?”

Modestly he told her he helped the Pickers, squashed a tonne of cans into a bale and Joe said he could buy it. He seemed to have finished so I added, “I think Sammy will be interested to know we saw the rolling roller and Electric Eddy as well”.

Granddad took over. He praised Joe for taking the time to show us round and complemented him for not being afraid to answer every question honestly.

Sammy listened and when he finished asked if we had seen the cardboard, glass and plastic being separated?

We hadn’t but Granddad uttered, “Erm, not sure”.

I wanted to say Joe might have told us Red Eye spots them. They are separated by a puff of air that sweeps them down tubes and they drop into bins. However, unsure of the details I said nothing.

Granddad looked awkward. He had realised Joe had not answered every question and we had not seen everything. He admitted the Red Eye Separator was in a tunnel and we couldn’t see it.

Sammy asked calmly, "What do you think happens to plastic when it goes in there?"

Granddad shrugged and said honestly, "I don't know, but I think it falls into a bin, gets squashed in the baler and stored in the warehouse until someone buys it".

Joe had talked about Red Eye with great respect but Sammy didn't. "Red Eye is great but there are some things it can't do. Did Joe tell you Red Eye can't see black?"

He didn't. We looked surprised so she explained, "If it can't see it, it can't pick it. If it can't pick it, it can go anywhere".

She made it sound important but I didn't understand why. I said thoughtfully, "Can't see black? What difference will that make?"

She explained, "The problem is if it can't see it, it can't pick it, and it can go anywhere. Try to imagine you bought a block of white plastic to make white bottles. You wouldn't be happy if your block had black bags in the middle. Your bottles would be black and white".

Granddad told her he had worked as a Picker at the MRF and he and the Pickers had removed dozens of black bags.

Without compromise Sammy stated, "It only needs one to get through!" then asked, "Did you get every black bag or did some get away?"

Granddad blushed and wriggled awkwardly. Clearly he didn't want to admit some did get away. She watched him and eventually he said, "Don't remember".

She scratched her head and stared. It made him wriggle again and added his excuse. "We picked everything we saw but might not have seen it all".

As though it was some sort of game she scratched her head again. He wriggled again but this time said nothing.

Determined to make him admit the problem Sammy gently asked, “How many?”

“Er” Granddad hesitated, “one or two”.

She had won. Even one black bag could spoil the bale. It could have gone anywhere. She asked, “Where did they go?”

“Er” Granddad hesitated and shrugged, “don’t know”.

Her nose twitched as she put her argument. “That’s the trouble, nobody knows. It is something that needs ironing out and that could take twenty years”.

She joked, “They’ll have to give old Red Eye a rub or maybe get a Black Eye Separator too. Those bags could have gone into the plastic and glass and the cardboard and contaminated everything. Because of a few bags everything will have black spots. Imagine black spotted milk bottles, black spotted cardboard boxes or worst of all black spotted windows. Letting blocks get contaminated is costly. Buyers will pay a good price for a block if it is clean. For other stuff they may make an offer but the really badly contaminated blocks come over here to be burned”.

We realised the seriousness of the problem. People put stuff in blue bins, it is separated, squashed into bales then, because of a black bag or two burned in the Waste to Energy plant. I felt shocked. All the time and effort separating stuff wasted. However the thought of a Black Eye to scan for black bags while Red Eye scanned for everything else made me smile.

Good at impossible questions, Granddad asked “What can be done?”

Sammy didn’t know. She answered, “Let me think about it”.

While she thought, we thought. Granddad must have thought about the Council list at the same time as me. We both said, "The list says no black pots but it should say no black bags as well!"

Glibly I asked, "Any more problems?" Sammy didn't answer. She stood up, put on her coat, hat and mask and gave a hand signal like a general leading her troupe, and we followed.

On the step outside the canteen she said we would have to wear safety gear. Granddad joked, "Red boots, pink mask and yellow coat?"

"Don't think you'd suit red, Granddad. I'll take you to the changing room and get you some modest black and blue. I'm sure you will feel more comfortable in them".

Changed and ready to begin the tour we followed Sammy. Outside the canteen she insisted we should walk to the corner and stop then asked,

"Are you ready for this?"

The incinerator and all the other buildings were round the corner and we definitely wanted to see them. We didn't know why she asked such a silly question and in unison we answered "You know we are!" Granddad added, "We have had a good meal, we've got our safety gear on. We are ready for anything!"

She bowed and told us to step forward and look round the corner, to our left. The sight stunned us. We gasped. Her question made sense. From the gatehouse the buildings looked big but this close to them they filled every bit of the view. An experience I could compare with the view of Edinburgh Castle. The sight of it made such an impression I would never forget the castle and would never forget the Waste to Energy plant.

Sammy laughed, "That's what happened to me first time. It surprised me and took my breath away. It still does, and I've worked here for weeks". Moving forward, acting as tour guide, she pointed to the building where wagons were dumping waste and a crane lifted buckets of it into an enormous fire. She said, "That is the Hall and that is the incinerator".

Another Hall, I said to myself. It is a very popular name.

Granddad whistled, "That pit is a very big open fire".

Sammy said, the fire must be fed day and night. It must never stop burning. It heats water to make steam and the steam makes electricity!

Granddad wanted to confirm he understood how it works and gave his description. "This is a Waste to Energy plant. You burn rubbish to make heat, it boils water into steam, and that makes electricity".

Sammy's whole body nodded in appreciation and she confirmed she would show us everything. She did a hand signal and a friendly order, "Come on!"

We should have followed but seeing the incinerator fire blazing and no black smoke confused Granddad, he didn't move. He stared up at the chimney and asked, "Where does the smoke go?"

Sammy replied, "Good question Granddad. We do make smoke and ash and electricity so I'll show you the process from beginning to end. Like in the MRF some bits are out of sight but it will give you a chance to use your imagination". She did her follow me signal and this time we all walked together, closer to the Hall, but not too close.

Granddad rubbed his hands, and joked, "I can smell the heat".

Sammy swung round, sniffed, and said, "I don't think heat smells. Maybe that smell is your hands roasting or you have a bit of dust up your nose!"

"Dust!" Granddad protested, "I know what dust smells like!"

Sammy pointed at a conveyor taking dusty grey ash from the incinerator to a huge pile, and shouted, "Dust!"

"It's ash. Dusty ash" Granddad said, "and look, that pile is a mile high. It reminds me of my Dust Man days. I moved loads of it".

Sammy called out, "Very dusty ash".

We gazed at the pile and Sammy casually mentioned she collects steel and recycles it. She explained tins that are put in the khaki bin drop into the incinerator fire and melt. The melted steel falls out with the ash and a huge magnet collects it before it gets to the heap.

Granddad cooly commented, "That's interesting".

I thought, how amazing, tins melt and the steel is collected. I didn't know that and asked, "Is it?"

She didn't answer my question but promised to point out things like the boiler, steam drum, spray drier and bog house.

We laughed, "Bog house!"

She gave the signal, we understood and we followed.

Walking slowly beside the building we felt the heat, smelled the smells and finally stood looking up at clouds rising from the chimney top. They were not the black smelly smoke and dust Granddad expected. The cloud looked clean. He shouted, "Excuse me! What have you done to the smoke? Shouldn't it be black or something horrible. Your smoke is white like a cloud. Do you have a different chimney for the smoke? Where is it?"

Sammy gave the impression she didn't know. She looked up, scratched her chin and went "Mmmm" then in a childish, shocked, high pitch, treasure hunt voice answered, "Must be somewhere!"

She spun round then pointed to the bog house and playfully accused it of stealing the smoke. "There" she yelled then, changed to her tour guide style and calmly explained the dirt from the smoke is knocked out in the bog house. Only steam and carbon dioxide go up the chimney and out into space. Granddad looked doubtful so she assured him, "It is very clean".

"All that fire and no smoke" Granddad said. "You burn tons of rubbish and make your own clouds. Does it rain much round here, Sammy?"

She laughed "The clouds just blow away. We don't get more rain than anywhere else. We only get our share".

She had explained why the smoke is clean and Granddad saw how the clouds billowed out of the chimney and disappeared into the sky. He had another question, "Where do you make the electricity?"

Sammy smiled, "You ask a lot of questions. You want to know everything". She turned, pointed to the highest part of a very tall building, made the hand signal and instructed, "Follow me. The steam turbine and generator are up there!" She led the way to a set of stairs that looked like steel cobwebs. She raced up the first flight, turned and stared as I tip toe gingerly upward.

"Come on!" she shouted, "if I can do it you can!"

That assumption had to be proven. I had difficulty getting from step three to four and Granddad hadn't started. Looking at the steel cobweb that hung down from one floor to the next I muttered loudly "It's shaky" and complained, "it might fall to pieces".

Sammy shouted, "The steps are vibrating. It is you that's shaky. When you get to the top you wont even notice. Come on!"

I considered walking down again backwards, but Sammy's assurance I might not notice the shakiness at the top inspired me and Granddad walking behind me left no choice. I kept going. There was no way back. He followed me step for step all the way to the landing then overtook me. He looked so confident striding ahead, it should have given me courage, but it didn't. The vibration had not stopped and to add to my concerns I heard throbbing, hissing, whirring and clanging noises above my head. Sammy called again. "Come on Freddy! You must see the view!"

While thinking I didn't want to see the view, especially if I had to look down, I shouted "Coming!" I'd never suffered vertigo but had the feeling I might.

"Stick together" Sammy ordered when I finally reached the top. She commanded "and you! Don't look down!" She watched to make sure I did as I was told then gave more instructions. "We must be careful. Take care not to touch anything. Those pipes are full of red hot steam from the boiler, and the machines are inside that steel armour in case they break".

In fear of possible danger I walked on tip toes and almost tripped over the steel lattice work flooring, which seemed to be floating. Sammy grinned and advised, "Don't do that. You are quite safe. The worst thing up here is the noise of steam driving the turbine and the generator rattling. So don't worry".

Granddad thoughtfully said, "As soon as she has shown us how to make electricity. I'll take you down".

Sammy quickly explained, "Electricity is made using a spinning turbine to turn a wire coil very quickly, inside a magnetic field".

I didn't understand and looking at the stairs I rushed to ask, "Is it time to go down?"

Granddad exclaimed gleefully, “Magnets! They are everywhere”.

Sammy took my arm, held me back, and said, “Magnets, steam, turbines, I know a funny sketch about making electricity. You will forget all your troubles and worries if we act it out”.

She shouted instructions. “Freddy, you be the steam and the turbine! Pump up and down with one hand and roll the other arm round and round. The quicker you pump and roll, the more electric you’ll make!”

“Granddad! You are the shaft attached to the turbine and the wire coil, stretch out your arms wide. Hold Freddy’s turbine elbow with one hand and your other hand is a coil”.

I still didn’t understand. It sounded silly.

Sammy continued, “I’ll hold my hands apart on opposite sides of your coil, Granddad. They’ll be the magnets. When we get going and the coil goes round you’ll see electricity. We might need some practice but you’ll soon have the turbine and the shaft racing round. Are you ready Freddy? Start pumping!”

I grumbled, “Do we have to do this?”

Sammy shouted, “Yes!”

Granddad liked doing silly things and said, “It is fun”.

The whole thing seemed ridiculous and I couldn’t stop myself making a blurting noise each time I pumped. Sammy was right, we did need practice. The first few turns sounded like an old steam engine. My turbine arm moved slowly as I found it incredibly difficult to pump with one arm and roll the other, but I got it. Granddad had no problem performing like a penguin doing back stroke but best of all, Sammy looked shocked. We were making electricity and her body twitched, jerked and twisted and didn’t stop until she dropped her hands and declared, “That’s how to make electricity! It’s shocking. I don’t know why I do it”.

Granddad shouted, “Because we wanted to know and you had to show us. Now I know, steam in, electric out!”

His simple explanation suited Sammy. He had not mentioned rubbish, but she didn’t mind and behind her mask she smiled and repeated Granddad’s very enthusiastic rap, steam in, electric out.

She sighed, “Now you know. Let’s go”.

We had come to the end of our tour and Sammy signalled to follow her, so we did, all the way to the canteen for a cup of tea. When we arrived the staff were flitting around, making sure the place was tidy. They had finished and getting ready to go home. Sammy said we should go but Granddad wanted a cup of tea and he always gets his way. He cheekily approached one of the ladies and asked, “Can I get you a cup of tea, young lady?” She took the hint. He politely asked if she would make three cups as his friends were in need of a drink too.

He seemed to be in jokey mood. Trying to make us laugh he wound his arm round and round and said, “I’m going to copy Sammy’s electrifying performance” and made silly faces. She added to the humour, wound her arm round his and rapped, “Steam in, electric out!”

Unexpectedly the canteen staff applauded and we sat down. Sammy admitted she felt nervous when we arrived. She had not shown anyone else round, we were the first. She said we made her relax and she’d had fun. Best of all she would be pleased to guide us round again. You never know what the future has in store and we might go back so I asked for her number and told her we would give her a call if we decide we wanted another tour.

“We don’t want anyone else” Granddad insisted. “No one can make electricity like you”.

She smiled, said she felt flattered and insisted we had acted our parts very well.

Granddad asked where she had learned that sketch?

She told us she was in the school theatre group and performed it for their parents. They thought they were mad because sixteen year olds don’t do silly things, do they? She added, “My parents probably think Granddads shouldn’t be cheeky either”.

This might be our last time together. I couldn’t think what to say but thought Granddad would say something, he didn’t. Sammy had a question. She asked us to tell her what we would remember about our visit and suggested I might remember the heat, dust and electricity.

I responded, “I don’t have to think. You have made me forget my fear of heights. Thank you”.

She asked Granddad what he would remember. There was a moment of suspense while he thought and even more suspense as he spoke very slowly. “I’ll remember red boots and pink mask and a very pleasant day, thank you”.

“A very pleasant day!” I echoed emphatically. “A wonderful day! Oh by the way, I’ll look out for a Black Eye Detector!”

In no hurry to leave we walked slowly to the gatehouse. Sammy took the opportunity to tell Granddad she had thought about how to stop rubbish getting into the recycled bales and had a suggestion. “You have a blue bin. Try something different, have many bins, red, white and blue ones. Put cardboard in one, glass in another and so on. It is called MULTI-STREAMING. Look it up on the internet”.

Granddad had something special, people do things for him that they wouldn’t do for anyone else. She had thought about his question and given her advice. We promised to take it and look it up on the internet. At the gatehouse we said our thanks and sad goodbyes. In those few hours touring the site she had been our guide and friend. We would remember her and I knew she would remember us. She made her excuses and left before Speedy arrive and Granddad and I agreed we would miss her.

Speedy arrived in the big blue car and Granddad asked if he could drive it. I trembled at the thought and Speedy explained he didn't own the car and couldn't let him drive it. Granddad looked disappointed, put on his miserable face, and Speedy change his mind. He let Granddad have a go on the understanding he would only drive on the private road and stop when he was told.

Sitting in the back, panicking, I asked myself why did Speedy agree to give Granddad a driving lesson? He could do it another day, when I'm not here. Fortunately Granddad didn't drive too fast and stopped when he was told. When Granddad swaggered, "Easy as riding a bike" I praised him and told him he made driving an electric car seem easy.

On the way home, shaking a lot less than I expected, we chatted about our wonderful day out and Sammy. When he said, "Knows her stuff" a hundred times I insisted he should stop complimenting her.

At home he thanked me for arranging our day out and chatted happily about Joe and Speedy and Sammy's idea about different bins for different stuff. He said he likes recycling. I laughed and told him he can use my blue bin. He laughed and told me had had bigger plans.

As he left I said, "See you tomorrow".

He said, "So long".

CHAPTER 9

Granddad never drops in, I hadn't seen him for years. He only called in because he found that list in his bin and he wanted me to explain it to him. I hoped that having fun visiting those sites would make him want to see me again. I had the cups ready, but he didn't arrive.

For a few days I told myself he will turn up, but he didn't. A week later I put his cup in the cupboard and gave up waiting. Sad and annoyed I told myself next time he turns up I wont be in. I wanted to forget about him but the bins were constant reminders. I told myself he was not coming back, I should forget about him so tried not to see the bins, avoid them and went out less often than usual. It took time. Problems go away and you don't realise for ages. That is what happened to me. My life was back to normal. I had completely forgotten about him, then one quiet morning I heard a noise. Someone was shuffling bins in the car port. Rushing to tell them off I opened the door and shouted, "What do you think you are doing?"

Granddad had arrived. I had missed him more than I could say. The feelings I had tried to let go danced to the rhythm of my heart thumping with joy and I wanted to hug him and say I forgave him for disappearing for such a long time, but my throat was dry and the words would not come.

Eventually I said crossly "Where have you been? I've been worried about you".

He smiled and cheerfully said, "No need to worry. I don't".

I shouted, "Well I do! I thought you got lost and I missed you".

He seemed to shrug and that maddened me. I shouted, "What are you doing?"

He had a project in mind and told me calmly, "Thought we can try Multi-Streaming, Freddy. I've brought these little bins. We can have a red one for cans, white for plastic and..." Before he finished I told him I have a bin for that stuff. It is blue.

"Blue" Granddad echoed. He reached out then said, "Big, isn't it? Nearly as tall as me, and at least three times bigger than my cute little ones".

"Cute but a bit small" I scoffed. "Wont get much in them".

He tapped one small bin and assured me "Just enough" and calmly carried on explaining his plan. "I thought we should try sorting stuff out for the Council. Make their job easier".

"Incredulous" I bellowed, "Easier! There can be nothing easier than emptying one bin every two weeks, the way the Council does!"

He stopped, looked at his poor little bins, turned thoughtfully to me and said, "Maybe not, however..."

He had not given up. I was about to tell him to pack up his little bins and stop wasting time but instead, held my breath and he continued. "But so much better for MRF. You saw me and the Pickers struggle to remove all the rubbish from the conveyor. I thought if there is only one thing, say glass, on the conveyor, the Pickers will have no trouble". To make his argument stronger he added a Granddadism, one of those things that only Granddad could say, "They will look and say, if it isn't glass, it is rubbish". He then suggested, "They wont need all the technology. They will be able to do all the separation work themselves. What do you think, Freddy?"

I thought some people say recycling doesn't work but the Pickers, Eddy, Red Eye and the magnet do a good job. It might not be perfect but nothing ever is. Tongue in cheek I said, “So should we put Eddy and the other equipment into retirement?”

He had said what he wanted to say so rattled the bins and avoided answering my question by reminding me Sammy had suggested Multi-Streaming. She had talked about it, but she didn’t say the Council will do it. Pretending to support his idea I humoured him. “Multi-Streaming, someone will appreciate that we have separated all the waste into tiny bins”. With a change of tone I said, “Just one problem, Granddad!”

He didn’t want to hear any problem. He looked at his line of bins, a little red one, the big blue one, a little white one and a yellow one, and put his hands over his ears.

I shouted, “The problem is the Council only collect blue bins, not red white and blue ones!” He turned, sneakily looked at my mouth to make sure I had stopped talking, and put his hands down. I had another complaint. “They look odd! The blue bin looks like a giant between little ones, why have you done that?”

He answered, “So you’ll find it easy to remember. The red is for aluminium, the blue is for cardboard and the white is for plastic”.

It did not make sense. I asked him to explain why I would find it easy to remember?

I had not noticed each bin had a giant sized label stuck on the front. He pointed to the ALUMINIUM, CARDBOARD, PLASTICS and GLASS labels, read them out, and exclaimed, “That’s why!”

I felt humiliated until I realised he had missed one very important thing. “Er” I said, “I don’t mean to embarrass you but where is the tin bin?”

“We wont bother with tins, Freddy. Sammy said tins are melted in the incinerator, so we can put them in the khaki bin. They wont be wasted, she will get them”.

I always put mine in the Recycling bin. I didn’t really understand his reason not to. He explained tins can be hard to clean and if they are not cleaned properly… He didn’t finish his sentence. “For example,” he said, “tomato soup and beef stew spoil any good clean plastic or even worse, cardboard”. He wrinkled his nose and said, “We wont bother with tins”.

My face turned purple as I thought of the reasons I should bother. They are on the Council list, I’ve always recycled them, changing the habit of a lifetime is really hard and I don’t want to give up. Sammy wouldn’t want me to. I’m not argumentative but I had to complain so took a deep breath and told him he would have to give me a better reason to stop.

He insisted he had given it a lot of thought it was a good idea. He said, “For example, sometimes, accidentally, there may be some left over stew in a tin. When it is thrown on top of cardboard it stains it. Stained cardboard can’t be recycled into anything, it has to be picked out”. He concluded “We wont ever get stained cardboard Freddy, because we will put all our tins in the khaki bin”.

I wanted to say I doubt I ever leave any food in my tins, I always clean them, however, once or twice I had rushed, given them a quick wash and couldn’t be sure they were absolutely clean.

He added, “We will be giving Sammy a present. She has a magnet at the Waste to Energy plant. She collects tins and we wont mark the cardboard because we will put our tins in the khaki bin”.

How could I argue? It felt revolutionary yet seemed sensible. There seemed to be several advantages. The little bins are nicer to look at, I wouldn't have to wash and clean tins so rigorously and it would be a doddle putting all the stuff in the right bin. Over all I liked his set up but didn't want to admit it so dithered and asked him to explain again why he thought it so good.

He said everything he could think of. Everyone accidentally stains cardboard sometime and putting tins in the khaki bin would avoid staining it. The tins would not be wasted, they be melted and the metal collected in Sammy's Waste to Energy plant. He also talked about colours and labels. "You should relate colours like red for Aluminium, but if you suddenly loose you sense of colour you can read the label".

Being as awkward as possible I said, "What if I can't read the label?"

Granddad sneered, "Turn the light on and put on your glasses!"

He continued, "Labels and colours will be two things to remind you what goes in which bin. The colours will attract your attention and your brain will connect colour and labels every time. You'll soon learn red for aluminium, yellow for glass and white for plastics".

He had won me over. Convinced I said, "What a good idea. I'll soon remember to put cardboard in the blue bin and tins in the khaki one, wont I?"

Granddad beamed, gave each bin a congratulatory tap, read out the labels, then to reassure himself that I would use his bins asked when we could start?

I had put off answering his question long enough and had to be honest. "I like your idea, Granddad. I hope everyone else does too. But you wont get the Council to change".

He disregarded my concern about the Council, said he would sort that out later but he wanted to practice dropping things in the bins. I had a tray full of stuff to be recycled, so we tried. We worked as a team. He had the boring job, pointing to the correct bin and giving me instructions. I had the fun job of throwing stuff in the bins. Although we spent a long time talking about what went into which bin I found it hard not to throw everything in the blue one. He had to remind me to put only cardboard in it. Without him I would have got it wrong, and would have had to pick it and put it in the right one.

Holding up a plastic bottle, the last thing on the tray, I decided to be kind, change roles, let him throw it in the bin and I would give instructions. He tried and discovered he is good at giving instructions but not good at taking them. I shouted "Plastics" and grinned like a Cheshire cat when he dropped the bottle in the glass bin. It amused me and it was hard not giggle watching him retrieve it and put it in the plastics one. We had finished and he announced, with great satisfaction, "Mission complete!"

I felt the satisfaction too. We celebrated with a high five. We looked down at the little bins and the celebration stopped. We had put everything from my tray in them yet they were half empty. Granddad picked each one up to check how heavy, or as he said, how light they were. He did some hand measurements to check how high, or as he said how low they were, and complained it would take weeks to fill them.

He waved the plastic bin in front of me and appeared to blame me. "This is the fullest one and it is half empty" he argued. "Have you hidden some stuff? Do you have another tray or have you put some in the khaki bin when I wasn't looking?"

His accusation did not seem funny. He knew the little bins were not full because we had divided all the recycling by four, and when you divide, things get smaller.

"Not much in there" I agreed, "it's everything I've collected while you've been away". I had nothing to hide but Granddad opened the khaki bin lid and quickly shut it again before the smell escaped. He had just enough time to assure himself I had not cheated. Shaking his head and pretending to be confused he muttered, "Not in there. Just rubbish".

He was being silly so I sarcastically thanked him and asked him "Please don't accuse me. If you find this frustrating we can stop now or you might feel better if you jump in the bins. You can squash the bottles and cans I wont mind".

He took great pleasure stamping up and down in each bin and when he finished observed, "Even less in those bins now".

The truth is they had the same stuff as they had before but there was a lot more empty space. It looked less because he had flattened it all. It made me think, if the bins get too full, I could call him to do his bin dance and make room for more recyclables. The bins would only need to be emptied when he couldn't get in them. It would take a long time. Granddad did new measurements with his hands and estimated it might take six weeks to fill a little bin. The Council would only need to call every six weeks. He also decided none of them would be very heavy so the Recycling Operatives would be able to lift those little bins and empty them, just like he used to do when he was a Bin Man.

I thought that will be good exercise for the Operatives and if they had a small electric wagon, instead of diesel, it would be good for the Planet too.

"Come on" I called, "after all that hard labour it is time for tea".

We washed our hands, remembering to rinse, soap and sing Happy Birthday then had tea and a chat. Sitting on the stool, the way he did before, looking out of the kitchen window he imagined his own Multi-Stream MRF in the back garden. We had fun working out a name for it. We considered lots of sensible names but decided it should be called, INSANE RECYCLING. Madness, I know but while we sat at the picnic table in the garden he pretended an electric wagon delivered tonnes of squashed cans. He dressed up to pick out the rubbish, with mask and gloves, and sorted them. He enjoyed playing but wanted to see the real thing, so at lunch time he looked for a Multi-Stream MRF on the internet.

"Useless!" he muttered angrily, after searching for an hour. "Modern technology, mythology, I'd say. Can't find one!"

"Give me five minutes" I shouted, "you have your tea and I'll look".

"You wont find one!" he grumbled, "there are no Multi-Stream MRFs on that computer. Don't waste your time!"

A few minutes later I said, "Some in America".

"I want one here!" Granddad protested, "I want to go to one right now!"

I had not found any locally or anywhere in England but there were lots in America. If he wanted to see one we would have to go.

Did I ever say he is awkward? He didn't want to go so to persuade him I told him it is the birthplace of recycling, without America we would be up to our ears in waste.

America is the land of opportunity and Disney World. It would be fun and I would take him if he would go!

I wanted to go and persisted, “It’s great, big, exciting and fun. You must take your grandson. I want to go”.

CHAPTER 10

The airport with all its distractions could not stop Granddad and me worrying we might get lost or catch the wrong plane. We checked in at two in the morning, four hours before departure time and still did not feel confident we would catch the right one. Boarding the plane Granddad asked if we would be given a badge or something for flying. Children might get a badge or a packet of sweets but we were too old for that. I told him he could have a seat by the window and look out at the Ocean, if he wanted.

Staring, at the blue sky, clouds and Atlantic Ocean he noticed the plane moved very slowly and soon discovered time seemed to fly if he ate snacks and watched videos instead. When we touched down in America I checked the Airport clock, it showed nine o'clock and my watch showed two. Either we had gone five hours back in time, travelled six thousand miles in three hours, or America has a different time to Britain. Another clock showed time around the world and American time is different. I tried to trick Granddad, told him we must have arrived before we set off but he had noticed the clocks and told me to put my watch right.

We had a bus to catch so we collected our baggage, followed the crowd out of the airport and dialled the hash and number for a taxicab to take us to the Greyhound bus station. Cab drivers are notorious for driving quickly and our driver must have driven faster than most. I will never get used to speed! He weaved in and out of the traffic so fast my hair stood up and Granddad's flat hat lifted off his head. We arrived in plenty of time and had large cups of coffee while we waited for the bus.

The seating in the bus was very comfortable, luxurious, and the driver drove steadily so I felt relaxed. Unfortunately Granddad kept saying, "We're lost!"

His nervous excitement reminded me of bus trips he took me on when I was a boy, Maude's Mystery Tours. I never knew where we were going, it was a mystery. With our bag of sandwiches and a bottle of pop I happily relied on Mr Maude. We had fantastic days out wherever he took us. Here, looking out at the vast emptiness, I had to rely on the driver and although I didn't know where we were, I knew we were on our way. Each time Granddad complained I crossed my fingers and said, "Stop worrying Granddad. We are not lost. We are on Route 66, the most famous road in America".

We travelled for hours in the comfort of the bus's temperature controlled air conditioning and admired the unusually bright sun and cacti which were growing in their natural environment, sand. It looked like a desert yet we expected it to be as pleasant outside as it was in the bus. We were not prepared for the unbearable heat.

When a huge building came into view we assumed it must be the MRF and stood on the step, beside the door. Feeling nervous and excited we couldn't wait to get off the bus and go. The bus stopped, the door opened, Granddad stepped forward, then back. The heat hit him. He yelled, "It's an oven out there!"

Fortunately Roy, our American guide and MRF owner was waiting at the stop with water. He handed out the bottles and advised, "Sip don't gulp" and said those magic words, "welcome to America".

Between sips we thanked him for the water and followed him to the air conditioning comfort of his truck. All the way to the site Granddad chattered. He told Roy about his experience at the MRF and Waste to Energy Plant in

England, everything we did at Joe's plant to what we did at Sammy's. He told Roy he enjoyed picking rubbish and wanted to get a feel for the job in an American MRF.

Roy looked amused and seemed to doubt he had done picking and enjoyed it. I quickly assured him it was true. Roy thought it over, shrugged his shoulders, and agreed he could. He warned "The hardest part is making the coffee". We thought he was joking and laughed.

As we entered the plant Roy told Granddad he would need to wear safety clothing. Granddad told him he was prepared, he had brought his own mask and gloves. Roy did not believe him and said, "And my horse is called SILVER".

I knew it was a joke about Roy Rogers, a movie star cowboy who wore a highwayman's mask, and his horse called Silver. Roy Rogers was a real hero. Every Saturday all the kids in town went to the cinema to see him beat the bad guys. Too old to go Granddad didn't see the movies and didn't know why Roy and I laughed when he said his horse was called Silver. He thought we were laughing at him with his mask, gloves and flat hat.

Anxious, to get started, he said, "Don't know what you are talking about. Can I get on that line?"

Roy made a sound like a horse, "Yeh!" Then explained, "Today is CAN DAY. The only thing on the conveyer will be cans. When you see anything that doesn't look like a can it is rubbish. Even gold nuggets have to go in the bin".

"Gold nuggets!" Granddad exclaimed. "You are joking!"

I wasn't sure if he meant it or not. In America anything can happen. I told him to keep his eyes open for gold nuggets and any other treasure.

All the Pickers were tall and Granddad looked small. They reminded me of AVATARS and Granddad did not look like an Avatar, even a small one. The others towered above him yet in his overall, boots, gloves and mask he looked professional, and if he hadn't worn his hat at a jaunty angle no one would have known it was him.

He felt privileged Roy told him to stand first in the line and called him Chief Picker. Determined to be the best Picker he watched very carefully for the conveyor to start and the cans to roll. Roy stood beside him and gave him advice, "First in line always finds the gold nuggets. Let me know when you find one?"

Granddad answered, "If one comes rolling down the line I will see it. I like spotting the rubbish nuggets, and I will let you know!"

Roy laughed, "Just remember to put the rubbish in the bin, but if it is gold let me know, so I can take it home". They finished the light hearted banter and Roy gave Granddad more serious advice. "The Chief Picker, that is you, has to check his team is ready". Granddad glanced at the professional Pickers behind him, thought they looked ready and nodded to each one. Experienced at working on the line they must have heard the hooter hundreds of times, however, they all jumped when it sounded and the belt rolled. The noise of cans bumping each other filled the air. Granddad grinned with excitement and stared as heaps of cans of every size, shape and colour flowed towards him. His body swayed deftly as his eyes scanned, looking for gold nuggets and rubbish. After an hour his grin had disappeared, he'd only picked a few straws and a crisp packet. He needed a break and a cup of tea. Roy came to his rescue. Before we left the building to go to the canteen Granddad chatted to his work mates, checked their bins and realised their bins were almost empty too.

All the way from the plant to the canteen Granddad said nothing. His silence was unbearable. I thought he's either in a mood or got a secret so asked him to tell me what he was thinking about. When he didn't reply I felt sure it must be a secret. The only way to find out would be to ask him lots of questions and hope he would answer one. When I asked if he'd had fun his face scrunched up miserably. He didn't have to say a word, I knew he hadn't and he was in a mood.

In the canteen Roy was keen to know how much rubbish Granddad had put in his bin and asked if he found anything interesting? Granddad didn't want to talk. He remained tight lipped until Roy finally forcefully asked, "Did you fill your bin?"

Granddad's unhappy face, sad eyes and pet lip and his disappointed response, "Americans are very tidy people, not much rubbish today" forced Roy to change his approach. His gold nugget joke would not be appreciated so he told him not to be sad and offered him a cup of tea. "You English always say a nice cup of tea. I will get you one".

CHAPTER 11

We watched Roy stride to the bar and saw him place his order with the assistant. There seemed to be a problem. He had a conversation with the manager then called, "Hey Granddad! They don't serve tea. I am embarrassed to say, they don't know how to make it".

Granddad hated not getting his own way. His face changed, his eyes squinted and with an angry stare looked ready to sulk, however, the rattle of beans in the blender and the strong coffee smell that wafted our way made him decide to have good old American coffee instead. Roy's embarrassment showed. Red faced he brought his can and our coffees to the table and insisted the staff do not know how to make tea and Granddad should teach them.

Avoiding the subject Granddad praised the staff for making excellent coffee. Grinning he said he could get to like it and he would be pleased to have coffee instead of tea. He made us laugh when he said, "I'll do it the American way".

Relieved, Roy tactfully suggested he might like to try some cool drinks sometime and told him, "Most Americans like cool drinks on hot days".

Granddad made him laugh, he said, "True Brits have a hot drink on hot days, in fact every day". The coffee, the chat, something changed the mood. Feeling better Granddad talked about our tour of the English MRF and the Waste to Energy Plant. Roy wanted to know why we had come to America to his Plant. "After all," he said, "picking rubbish must be about the same here as it is in Great Britain".

Granddad assured him picking in Britain is very different. "Picking is much more fun when you're busy" he said. "Over there I soon filled my bin, but here it will take weeks".

He had not answered the question, he did not say why we had gone to America, so I did. "We came here because Granddad wanted to see a multi-stream facility where customers put recyclables into different bins. Back home in Britain we don't have one. We have the big blue bin Single-Stream system. We put all our recyclables in it and the Council take it away".

Roy had worked in England and told us he knew about British blue bins and mixed up waste. "You Brits co-mingle cardboard, glass, tins and cans in one blue bin. Some places do that. We don't. Our customers separate everything so we don't have to. We just clean out any rubbish from one thing at a time. Some say it is slower but I say it is cleaner. Today we sort aluminium. It is CAN DAY".

Hoping he would share his opinion I asked, "Which way is best, single or multi?"

He considered my question then asked, "Why do I do this job? This is a Material Recovery Facility so I recover cans, cardboard and other stuff. In this process I don't waste much and all my bales are clean. It takes a little longer but hey, I like to give my customers the best. Customers who buy my bales save money, materials and power". He lowered his eyes then said, "But if I was in a rush… that's another thing. I guess it depends".

He had not committed to either system. I couldn't argue but felt his way sounded best. I told him about Sammy's suggestion to try Muti-Streaming and how we had sorted my recyclables at home, into separate bins.

"Did you?" he asked, "And what did you think?"

Although the bins had not been emptied and checked for rubbish by anyone else I answered without hesitation, "It worked a treat".

He chuckled, "Great, if you were not so far away you could bring your stuff to my plant". He smiled and confessed, "I'm only joking. I'm sure you will have done it right and it wont need sorting. Everybody wants to save the world but so many people can't even get Single-Stream stuff right. They want to save the world so badly they put everything in the blue bin. They don't realise much of it has to be picked out and burned. Some are even worse, they don't want to do any recycling, they object, and leave it to others. The conscientious ones can be trained but the objectors will never learn".

I understood his message, people who want to do the job properly can be trained and others cannot. Maybe the best way is only train the ones who want training. I had great respect for Roy and happily chatted to him for ages. I listened to his assertion his bales are worth more than British ones and wondered if he really does get top price for them?

While we talked Granddad fidgeted and observed other people in the canteen, so when Roy finished his can and went to the bar for another one, I told him to stop it. He refused and said he was learning the American way. He confided he had discovered why the Pickers found so little rubbish in the waste. He whispered, "The Pickers told me all the cans come from businesses, shops, pubs, clubs, cafes, canteens and reverse vending machines so they don't expect much rubbish!"

That explained why there was so little rubbish but I had never heard of a reverse vending machine. It sounded like a wind up. I asked him to tell me about them?

Without a smile he said, "They are machines that pay you for your empty cans".

Trying not to laugh I asked, "Did the Pickers tell you any other jokes?"

He looked aghast and insisted they are real.

"Don't be silly!" I said, "They can't be real or we would have them in England". Then doubtfully, "Wouldn't we!"

Granddad nodded towards the canteen door and whispered, "You think I'm joking. I swear I'm not. That is one over there".

I stared, the machine looked like an everyday vending machine, the ones that vend cans in England. I shook my head sympathetically.

With a very stern look he pointed to the machine and explained, "You don't put money in and get a can out, you put a can in and get money out. I've been watching people do it. We need a can and I will show you".

There was nothing I could do to change his mind. He needed to show me, but to demonstrate he needed a can.

With a look and an angry whisper he commanded, "Find an empty!"

We looked everywhere, including the waste bins, but couldn't find one, which seemed odd. People we had seen at tables must have cleared their cans away. I groaned, "They are so tidy". I did notice Roy took his can back to the bar but still asked, "What did Roy do with his?" then quickly added, "He will have another one. We will have to ask to borrow it".

As expected, Roy returned with another can. Like two unprofessional secret agents we watched his every movement. He noticed our suspicious behaviour but instead of asking why we were watching him he asked if his hat was on straight. Of course we realised he suspected we were up to something and decided to ask if we could put his empty into the reverse vending machine for him?

To my relief he enthusiastically said, "Great idea! Everyone who works here uses it. I had it installed so I can save every bottle and can. No one ever puts straws in the can either. They have to be empty because it works on weight. If it is too heavy it might not pay out. People are very careful". He quickly finished his drink and handed me his empty can. We rushed to the machine. I dropped it in the draw and Granddad collected the money. "Feels like pocket money" he said as he rattled it in his hand. He explained when he was ten he earned his pocket money collecting lemonade bottles and returning them to the lemonade man. Those bottles were used over and over again.

We had our fun. Granddad proved the machine paid for empty cans and had a hand full of dimes. He offered them to Roy but he insisted we had earned them, we could keep them as a souvenir. "Take them back with you and frame them" he said, "Put my name on them. I'll sign them if you want".

Back on the line Granddad had a very boring time picking but told himself it is not just cleaning the waste it is cleaning the environment and every bale will bring top price, because it is clean. The bright spots, break times, he talked to the Pickers and seemed to be making friends with them all.

CHAPTER 12

Granddad and the Pickers finished work and we went to our room. I asked him if the Pickers talked about their kids, sport and all the things normal people talk about? His slow response gave the impression he would keep it a secret but his face soon changed, he beamed and told me the whole team wanted to know his life story.

They asked his age, where he works, what he does for fun, that sort of thing. He said he told them he couldn't remember his age but he works at the Palace and empties the Royal bins. Only Granddad could tell such a blatant lie and be believed. He carried on with his story and told them he once found a crown in one. The Queen thanked him personally for being honest and returning it. She told him it is the one she wears at Christmas, her Christmas crown. Even I knew he meant it came out of a Christmas cracker.

"Funny thing is," Granddad said, "they laughed when I told them we sorted your recycling into little bins. You know they train their customers to sort their own recycling. They said it takes weeks before it clicks and they know what to do. We saw today, the customers nearly always get it right, a straw or two maybe, but not much else. I think it proves it pays to educate the customer".

He hadn't told me what American Pickers talk about so I asked, "What did they say about children and cars?"

"Cars" he said, "everyone has one. Children! Brent has two sons. They want to start a sorting business. He advised them not to take kerbside waste because people like you and me sometimes get it wrong. We know, don't we, Brits put rubbish in the recycling, so do Americans. It's the same the whole world over. He told them to do what Roy does, collect recycling from Businesses. It is cleaner".

I agreed, collecting clean waste makes sense. Roy's plan works. He told me his bales are always clean, never rejected and always get the best price. He could be making lots of money. Granddad had discovered how clean American business waste is. It is so clean it is boring but if you want to make money be bored, get rich and let someone else collect the duff stuff.

We had travelled 6000 miles to learn the tricks of the trade. The oddest thing being the reverse vending machine. I asked what the Pickers had said about them?

"Those machines" Granddad said. "Roy has invested in lots of them right across the county. They are a nice little earner. They sound like a good way to make easy money so I asked if we should buy one and take it to England? Brent told me if they were allowed in England Roy would put them everywhere, but they are not allowed".

Under my breath I said to myself, the rules need looking at.

After a hard days' work Granddad was ready for a meal and thanked heaven we were in America, land of the giant T-bone steak and fries. We shared a meal and enjoyed every bite then went back to our room to watch TV. Looking for something appealing we flicked through thousands of channels but didn't find anything interesting so we sat in rocker chairs, on the porch, and watched the sun go down.

Next morning we had breakfast in the hotel restaurant. The waiter offered us coffee and water melon for breakfast. He claimed to be shocked we'd never tried it. "It is healthy" he said. "The chef thought you would like a healthy breakfast before you go for your morning run".

The idea of going for a run any time struck me as absurd, just as silly as water melon for breakfast, but I thought I should not laugh in case it offended him. Not sure if the waiter was having fun with us I decided to have some fun of my own. I said, “We usually have peas and avocado, but we’ll try the melon, thank you”.

When we finished, the waiter politely asked if we enjoyed the meal and although we knew it is part of his repertoire to make the customer feel good we suspected he wanted a tip. Unfortunately my suggestion to try the water melon was not what he was looking for so Granddad gave him a few dollars. He took the money, said, “Have a good day” and hurried to the kitchen.

Watching him until he disappeared Granddad said, “Smart young chap”.

I disagreed and argued “What! He should have known we Brits have breakfast cereal not melon! He is not a very good waiter and has a very unusual accent”.

Granddad claimed he had not noticed the accent and continued to describe him as smart. I remembered he told me he used to be in the army Awkward Squad. I used to think he was joking but now thought they trained him well. He liked the water melon and hoped we could have it again.

Reluctantly I accepted Granddad is always right and because he always gets his way, felt sure we would.

The early morning air, cool and fresh, made Granddad feel ready to work and me to watch. At the sorting bay he put on his Picker’s uniform and stood in line and I kept out of the way.

Roy arrived, greeted the Pickers, announced “CARD DAY” and asked Granddad to push the button. Thrilled to be given responsibility he gladly pushed it. The hooter tooted and the conveyor creaked into action. Granddad called out “Let’s get this show on the road!” and began sorting.

The way Roy said Card Day made it feel like another day on the calendar, another day of the week. When the belt started he didn't need to explain, it is the day for sorting cardboard.

After years of experience and training the Pickers had developed their skills. They could spot the slightest mark or stain on card and threw it out.

Watching Granddad, a novice, with very little practice, it amazed me and made me proud to see him jumping backwards and forwards examining every piece, throwing marked card into his waste bin and enjoying himself.

When Roy returned he looked in Granddad's bin and dramatically stepped back, as if shocked to see all the stuff in it. He exclaimed, "Horrible stains! They are disgusting!"

I tried not to laugh but his performance amused me. He didn't mind me laughing and continued to point at the stuff and give his opinion. "Those stains are disgusting. The trouble is cardboard stains so easily. It happens all the time. When I find who did it I will give them more training". He then identified each mark. "Look" he said, "coffee, tomato, steak, hot dog, hamburger and fries".

Granddad questioned, "I thought you said your customers are clean?"

"All except the messy ones" Roy laughed. "Some people do not appreciate how delicate cardboard is. I'll have to give someone a lesson. Maybe teach them to keep their coffee in a cup and food on a plate. If that stuff got into a bale..." He didn't finish his sentence. He just said, "Come on! You deserve a break".

CHAPTER 13

"Coffee?" Roy asked, as we stood at the bar. "Or you could have a juice and put the can in the reverse vender. I'll have it recycled for you".

More money in the bank for Roy, I thought. We pay a deposit when we buy the bottle and get it back when we reverse vend it, but he gets paid for returning the empty to be recycled. Easy money!

When Roy identified the stains earlier I recognised Granddad's knowing look. Roy said fries, Brits call them chips. He would have to tell Roy so it was no surprise when we sat with our coffees and juice that Granddad announced, "Fries! We Brits call them chips".

Unmoved, as though he had been expecting the correction and prepared his annoying response Roy smiled and said, "I know!" He gave Granddad time to think about it then said, "I know. Ella Fitzgerald sang about the odd way you guys talk, but I don't think she mentioned chips".

Granddad knew the song. He smiled and said, "Let's call the whole thing off".

I wanted to say touché but Roy talked with Granddad. He said, "Card Day! How do you like sorting card, Granddad? I notice you've been busy. Your bin is full. You must have had lots of fun".

"Most of it is marked with a small dot of something someone dropped accidentally. I'm not letting any accident, no matter how small, go through. Chunks of cardboard fit loosely in the bin so a little cardboard, about five kilograms, and a lot of fresh air, soon fill one. If I jump on it there will be more room".

"Five kilograms," I said thoughtfully, "that much would fill my blue bin. It took him an hour to collect five kilograms. At home in England it would take me half a year".

Before coming to America we visited the Waste to Energy plant, where all khaki bin waste is burned, but Granddad wanted to know if the same happens to waste cardboard in America. He asked, "Does cardboard we reject go up in smoke, or can it be recovered?"

I reminded him, "In England the smoke is filtered and washed clean in the Bog House".

We all giggled at the word Bog House, then Roy said, "So it should be, they have to stick to the regulations to stop the nasties going up the chimney".

Granddad seemed to hope Roy had a miracle cure for rubbish. He asked, "What do you do with the rubbish, Roy?"

Roy confirmed again there is nothing he can do with dirty, stained, stuff. He said, "Regrettably I have to get rid of it. The stains wont wash out, no one wants it so it has to be burned in the Waste to Energy plant. I hate to send anything there because burning doesn't just create smoke, it creates the dreaded GREENHOUSE GAS, carbon dioxide,".

"Greenhouse Gas?" Granddad asked naively. "What is that?"

I couldn't think how to describe it and Roy had never met anyone who didn't know. He was lost for words.

Granddad couldn't wait for our explanation and talked about the greenhouse he used to have on his allotment, may years ago. He assured us it worked very well full of fresh air and compost.

We smiled and I humoured him. I told him I remembered he made a concoction of grass cuttings, rotting vegetation, weeds, peel and leaves and called it compost. His grass cuttings and weeds were so valuable he wouldn't give them away.

He wanted to know if gardeners fill their greenhouses with greenhouse gas to make the plants grow? It amazed me how out of touch Granddad was. He didn't seem to know anything about environmental problems.

Roy gave him a simple explanation. "You will have been told a couple of things at school. The sun shines and warms the World. Air contains Carbon Dioxide (CO2), a gas that holds the heat. Burning stuff makes more carbon dioxide. It is a greenhouse gas. More of it holds more heat and creates Global Warming. It is bad. That is why I like nice clean recycling and don't like to send stuff to the Waste to Energy plant. We need to cut down burning stuff".

Granddad remembered I told him about Global Warming and whispered he could see recycling properly is so important. He winked, in a reassuring way and said, "Less waste, less burning, less burning, less warming. We will get it right and help save the Planet".

We finished our drinks and Roy posted his empty can in the reverse vending machine. Oddly, seeing the money drop into the cup reminded Granddad again that he earned his pocket money collecting and returning empty lemonade bottles.

Back at the sorting bay the team had emptied all the bins ready to be filled again. Granddad pushed the button, the belt brought an endless stream of cardboard, and the sorting began, again. He did not complain, he enjoyed working hard, sorting cardboard. At lunch time Roy shouted. "Hey Granddad! Your bin is full. It's time for a break".

Granddad stopped the belt and commented, "Time flies when I'm busy".

"Cuppa coffee Granddad?" I asked at the bar. "I think you like American coffee". I scanned the room for a table and because I like something familiar told him "We sat over there". He didn't look, he watched the crowd of Pickers who arrived and sat at the opposite end of the room. "You're doing it again!" I whispered, "People watching!"

Roy noticed and asked him if he wanted to sit with us or them. Pleased to be given the choice he pointed and answered, "We've worked together all morning. I'm a Picker so if you don't mind I'll sit with the team".

"Are you sure?" Roy asked. "They are very noisy".

Granddad grinned, took his coffee, strolled across the room and joined them.

Sitting at our usual table Roy told me how his dad got him into the recycling business. His dad told him he would make a fortune picking rubbish. He didn't want to do it but his dad bought him a ticket to go to England and he got a job working in a Single-Stream Material Recovery Facility. He learned the hard way, on the line, and discovered customers accidentally or on purpose put all sorts of things in the blue bins. He had never seen so much rubbish.

He blamed the customers. I told myself his complaint did not seem fair. Customers like me have never been trained yet we are expected to know what to do. Granddad and I, with our DIY recycling, followed the list, but could not be sure we got it right.

Roy continued to complain. He said there is a whole spectrum of recyclers. He called them Rubbish, Perfect and In-Betweeners. He said Rubbish Recyclers are people who don't read the label and throw in any old rubbish. Perfect Recyclers are really keen. They care, read the label and when they are sure it can be recycled drop it in the blue bin. They wont do it unless they are sure. Sadly they often pop in a few extra things just in case. In-Between Recyclers do their best and sometimes get it wrong. The result is a mixture of good recycling and bad rubbish and that is why Pickers are needed. He and the other Pickers did their best but couldn't spot everything and what they missed went into the bales. He learned clean bales are worth a lot of money, they get top price, but contaminated ones are not worth much. If there is too much contamination in a bale it is sent to be burned at the Waste to Energy plant which is conveniently built next door.

The idea of collecting recycling, sorting it, baling it and then burning it horrified me. It does not make sense to do all that work for nothing. My face must have shown how I felt and Roy finished with, "Don't do it Freddy. Be like me, go for the easy life. Collect waste from shops and cafes where staff are trained and don't mix anything".

He based his advice on years of experience. He started as a Picker's mate and had to share a bin with someone more experienced. When it was full he wheeled it to a bigger bin and emptied it. When that bin was full a couple of older lads wheeled it to the incinerator. The place smelled and he used to pray for rainy days to wash the smell away. Rainy and windy days were best because the smell was washed and blown away. In a couple of years he became a qualified Picker. He didn't like the place where he worked so he moved. He moved several times but never found a good place. The Pickers were great but the places were rubbish. Some of the other Pickers talked about setting up their own facility. The idea appealed to him so he went home to the States and set up his own MRF business.

He admitted, "I guess it was good experience. I wouldn't be where I am now without it, and I like being here. I'm doing some good".

He had complained about his dad sending him to learn the trade and seek his fortune. Maybe Roy thought he could have found him something easier, but sometimes the easier job turns out to be dead boring. He would not have liked that. He liked being his own boss and it would not have happened if he hadn't started as a Picker's mate, would it? Maybe his dad was right. My Granddad used to say, where there's muck there's money. Comparing Roy's past with my own I thought if I had listened to Granddad I might have had more success, a business of my own, successful and rich.

Without sounding nosy or intrusive I asked, "How is the old man? Is he pleased with how things have turned out?"

Roy responded right away, "Yeh, he's fine, sits on the back porch in his rocker, singing to the stars and thanking God his son is doing well. I guess I thank God he's OK too".

He paused, obviously reflecting on his past, and watching the Pickers across the room, and told me he learned a miserable team does a miserable job. He is determined to keep his team happy. He wants them to wake up in the morning and look forward to going to work. They are well trained, get free coffee and he gets them the cleanest stuff to sort. They are happy. As if to prove him right there was a burst of noise from the other side of the room. Roy commented. "Sounds fun. That's what I mean".

Turning back to me he confided, "They are the best, quickest sort team in America. They can sort quicker than me". He smiled, "They don't know how good they are, and I wont tell them. Don't want it to go to their heads".

I believe a boss that appreciates his workforce has got to be a good boss. I wondered if he knew how good he is? He stopped to watch his team then, apologised. "Sorry, got carried away. I was saying… I've told them when they wake in the morning they should think Monday is Can Day,

Tuesday is Card Day. It is not complicated, it is one thing at a time, anyone can do it!"

Roy's story fascinated me. I couldn't wait to tell Granddad everything. Break finished, but there was a lot more sorting to do and no time to talk. I would have to tell him later. He and the other Pickers stood on the line and worked hard sorting mountains of cardboard and filling bins with piles of rubbish. When they finished Granddad must have still hoped the waste cardboard would be reprieved and Roy would tell him he had found some use for dirty cardboard. He asked what he does with it?

Roy pointed to half a dozen big metal cage-like containers full of marked cardboard and sighed, "We fill them and take it to be burned. I hate to burn it but have to accept there is no choice and console myself knowing the Waste to Energy plant does the world a favour, it makes electricity".

He sighed then protested, "I'm doing it, a favour! They don't do it for free! They charge for each cage. It costs me a fortune!"

"It's only rubbish" Granddad said, "I used to burn mine on the fire at home".

We had talked to Joe about open fires. I had googled smoke and smog and found Parliament passed a Clean Air Act to stop people burning stuff on open fires to stop things like that. Sammy told us stuff is burned in the Waste to Energy plant and the smoke is cleaned in the Bog House. However we found clean smoke, water and carbon dioxide is damaging the environment. Roy continued protesting. "Burning is not cheap. There are six cages full of rubbish and I have to pay to have each one burned!"

All his life Granddad had tried to cut costs, do things as cheaply as possible, and when Roy finally told him how much he would be charged he determined to save him some money. At home he had jumped in the little bins and made lots of space, he planned to do the same in the cages. If he jumped hard enough and squashed the air out of the first five the team would fill the spaces he made in each one with cardboard from the sixth one. In the end the five would be full and the sixth one empty.

No one doubted he would do it. The team clapped their support while he scrambled into the cages and did his dance. He jumped on the card until it would not go down any further and the team filled the spaces he made with card from cage six. Finally five cages were full and the sixth one empty. Roy only had five cages to pay for. When he finished, the team applauded and Roy shook his hand gratefully for saving him money and promised him a treat.

Granddad had made his mark. He would always be remembered telling his story, picking rubbish, and doing his flattening dance on top of the cages. I wished I had a picture but I'd missed the opportunity, he wouldn't be able to do it again because we had to go home tomorrow. This would be our last night in America, tomorrow we were due to leave to go back to England.

CHAPTER 14

Back at the hotel we had packing to do but Granddad couldn't concentrate. He didn't put one thing in his case. He felt too excited and danced round the room chanting, "I've been promised a treat".

With Roy's promised treat on his mind he couldn't stop dancing and when I reminded him we had to go he responded with a very energetic flattening dance and a quick Highland Fling. Without stopping, he suggested the treat might be a party, a leaving do, and he might get a leaving present. Feeling a twinge of jealousy I had spiteful thoughts like Roy has work to do, he wont have time to stop for you, you'll be lucky to get a recycled can and a cardboard box. Sometimes it is the way you say something that gives meaning to the words. "Might not!" sounded spiteful enough. He continued to dance and I could not stop myself having one last dig. I said, "You might get a can and a box of chocolates"

I instantly regretted saying it. He told me to stop being miserable and called me a party pooper. He accused me of trying to dampen his spirits and I wasn't going to succeed. I decided to try a different, more pleasant approach, and began to dance. Surprisingly I enjoyed it and shouted, "Is this cheerful enough for you?"

I'm not sure if I'd left it too late or he found my dancing embarrassing, he stopped and began to pack. In a very orderly fashion he put his underwear at the bottom, shirts on top and stuffed socks and handkerchiefs down the side.

When I stopped he had a pair of rolled up socks in his hand and I had the feeling he wanted to talk. I expected him to comment on my performance so held my breath and waited. He didn't say anything about me, he talked about

Roy. He complimented his modesty, success, Recycling Business and the way he treats his Pickers. He said, "All the Pickers respect him. He gives the impression he knows everything but doesn't show off. He is likeable, friendly and fun. It was his idea to do one thing at a time and forget about Monday and Tuesday days of the week, and talk about Can Day and Card Day instead. Pickers prefer those names, it's their code. No one else knows what they are talking about".

Chatting, as Granddad likes to do, he talked about giving bins and recyclers a name. "Think of a name for a bin, a nice friendly name. People are always nice to their friends. What about BeeBee or Freddy or…"

Not sure if he intended to flatter me or insult me and because bins always remind me of him, it seemed an obvious choice to call mine Granddad. I remembered Roy called recyclers Rubbish and Perfect and told Granddad. He laughed and acted bad-tempered, had a tiny tantrum, stamped his foot, shouted "Wont do it. Can't make me!" Sat on the floor, sulked and squealed for a minute then, threw his socks across the room.

I complemented him for acting like a rubbish recycler but noticed his eyes glazed when I said if his socks were supposed to be rubbish they had missed the bin. Head down he walked to the far side of the room picked up his socks, waved them then strutted to his bag and packed them.

Looking at me with a big grin he said, "Perfect!"

I assumed he meant a Perfect Recycler. Trying to sound sincere, not sarcastic I said, "Of course you are Granddad, in every way, but did I tell you Roy laughed when he said, perfect. He was joking. Perfect Recyclers are the people who know the Council want steel tins so throw in steel nuts and bolts and a bicycle chain. Pickers have to sort them out".

Referring to the painting he found at Joe's MRF I asked if the artist who put it in the Recycling bin could be described as rubbish or perfect? He didn't answer so I gave my idea. "They might have thought someone would finish it. That would be perfect. No one will finish it so it is rubbish. They should not have put the painting or vase in the blue bin and you would not have had to pick it out. They should have put it in the khaki one!"

Tired of fooling around Granddad shouted "Food! Let's go to the canteen".

Walking through the restaurant door he spotted the waiter we called Melon. He slyly nudged me and whispered, "Melon".

I did not see the man and thought that was another funny question. I didn't want any so told him, "You might remember we had some for breakfast".

He nudged me again and whispered, "Melon is on reception".

Melon, our breakfast waiter, a stout, balding foreign gentleman, we secretly nick named Melon because he served melon for breakfast, stood waiting to receive us and direct us to a table. "Hello" Granddad called cheerily. "Do you have a table?"

Melon rubbed his hands together and said, "A table will soon be free, if you didn't mind waiting".

That accent, I said to myself, is very unusual. I looked at Melon then the floor and thought, you've made it up. No one talks like that.

We were not in a rush, had lots of time, so Granddad surprised me when he protested. "What if we do mind waiting?"

I wondered if he misunderstood Melon's question or was he winding him up? Whatever he was up to I was concerned we might get nothing for breakfast tomorrow, so nudged him.

Melon looked at Granddad, trying to decided if he was a trouble maker or an elderly stroppy teenager with an open necked shirt, then began to explain. His explanation involved lots of funny head and hand gestures and although we couldn't understand the language had the idea he said, on the other hand, many times. We involuntarily responded with our own gestures. In any other circumstance we would have laughed but kept straight faces as we watched and listened and nodded each time he did.

Melon argued then set off to the kitchen. He stopped briefly at every table on his way, speaking to the diners who couldn't understand him either. Some feeling sympathetic, waved and nodded, did thumbs up and down and some, who looked as if they had seen his tantrum before turned away and ignored him.

Contrary to my expectation Melon soon returned from the kitchen and ushered us to a long table.

"Two" I muttered, "we don't need a big table, thank you".

"You sit" Melon said, "you need this very big table".

This had to be a wind up, two people at a table for twelve. He persisted. The more I argued the more certain he seemed to be we must sit at that table. Eventually I asked him to tell me which chair he would like me to sit on? "You sit where you like Mr Freddy, also you Mr Granddad".

Attempting to point out to him the table was too big for two I said, "This is a big table. Big enough for a party of…" Bizarrely I couldn't stop myself waving my hands and copying his funny accent. Suddenly I realised what I had said, this could be a party! It didn't matter how big the party could be it dawned on me this could be Granddad's leaving do.

Roy had not mentioned it to me, and Granddad had said nothing about it. It could be a surprise party. I stopped complaining and politely asked, "Are we celebrating tonight?"

"You are" Melon said, "big celebration, lots of peas and avocado".

Roy arrived and Melon beckoned him to come and said, "Mr Roy, the honoured guests arrived earlier than you".

Roy had arrived with the Pickers. Before he sat down he reached over the table and shook our hands then turned to Melon and thanked him.

Melon accepted the thanks and nodded.

Roy asked Melon if he had explain this is a celebration?

He nodded and Roy announced, "These two guys came all the way to America to learn from the best. It has been my pleasure to train them but now they are leaving us. This party is their treat".

Turning to Granddad Roy said, "I don't want to make a long speech. I want you to know having you around has been fun. We'll remember you on the line and in the cages". He handed Granddad a parcel and said, "I'm pleased to present you with this box of chocolates".

I grinned, a box of chocolates, an inexpensive box of chocolates.

Roy had not finished, he handed Granddad an envelope and told him it was a very special leaving present that he hoped would help him to achieve what he wanted, to become an Altruistic Recycler.

Holding out the very large envelope Roy added, "You must not open it until you get home!"

Granddad agreed he would wait and open it at home.

When the party finished Roy offered to escort us to our room in case someone tried to steal the envelope and arranged to take me and Granddad to the bus stop in the morning. I assured him I would be Granddad's bodyguard and no one would try to steal it.

In the room Granddad put his precious envelope in his bag which he zipped up and hid under the bed. I don't know if he slept, but when I woke in the morning he was staring at it.

"Is your envelope still there?" I asked facetiously, "You didn't post it anywhere, or put your name on it and post it to yourself did you?"

He opened his bag to check then zipped it up and grumbled, "Of course it is!"

I told him he didn't need to watch it all the time and explained it would be embarrassing watching him, watching it, on the bus, on the plane and train. Other passengers may think he is guarding the crown jewels.

"More important to me than crown jewels" he muttered, "it's going to help me start my Recycling Business".

We had melon for breakfast. I got used to it, quite enjoyed it, however I found it distracting watching Granddad staring at his bag, on the table, and was pleased when Roy arrived to take us to the bus stop. We didn't expect the Pickers to turn up, but they did. Hand shakes, high fives, slaps on the back and invitations to call again, almost made me cry.

On the bus Granddad clutched his bag with one hand and with the other waved furiously out of the window until Roy and the team were dots in the distance. I suggested we could sit back and relax, "No tears just happy thoughts". Granddad agreed.

From the bus to the taxi, to the plane and the train the bag could not have received more attention if it had been getting heart surgery. Arriving at the local station we hailed a taxi and I flung my bag into the footwell, dragged myself onto the passenger seat and fell asleep.

The driver woke me outside my house. I had slept all the way. Assuming Granddad was in the back, asleep, I shouted. There was no reaction, no sound so I shouted again.

"I'm not Granddad," the driver said, "I'm Al. I don't know why you're shouting".

The back seat was empty. Granddad had disappeared.

Tea for one, I told myself and put my Old Codger cup on the kitchen island and filled it. Some days, hoping he would turn up, I put both cups out, but always ended up telling myself tea for one.

I didn't know why he had disappeared. It was strange not having him around but I determined not to call him, he would have to call me.

His little bins reminded me of him and I conscientiously separated everything the way he wanted. Slowly but surely the bins filled and I wished he would come and do the bin dance.

I was ready to blame him if they got too full and I had to put all my recycling in the Blue Bin. I wanted to, but my conscience would not let me. I had to be faithful to him. When a bin was full I attempted to do a one foot flattening dance to make some space but had to finish with a ten pound hammer. It worked. I thumped it down, filled it up and thumped it down again until no matter how hard I thumped there was no more space. I had to put stuff into bags. After several months and many sleepless nights there were far too many bags. One day, tired and irritable I told myself I had been faithful to Granddad's Multi-Stream Recycling dream long enough. I determined to put all the bags in the blue bin, tomorrow.

CHAPTER 15

Tomorrow came and I could not do it. He would want me to keep up the good work so I continued separating my recycling into Granddad's red, white and blue bin collection and pouring stuff into bags. I liked the little bins and had no trouble separating my waste but worrying kept me awake. What could I do? Knowing the Council will only empty the big blue bin the only solution seemed to be mix all the recycling, throw everything on top of the cardboard. Again, several times, I put off till tomorrow, until tired, worn out, yet still hoping Granddad would come back, I began.

To start, the cardboard needed to be squashed with my ten pound hammer. The cardboard crumpled under the pressure and lay flat on the bottom of the bin. Pounding was hard work and I was worn out when I stopped. Going against Granddad's wishes would make me feel guilty so hoping that adding a little bag of something would only cause me a little guilt I chose a very small bag of jars.

About to pour them on top of the cardboard I apologised to Granddad, told him I love him, told him if he had come back sooner I wouldn't have to do this and told myself to get on with it. The bag was not heavy but the weight of guilt made me lift it slowly.

Unexpectedly everything went black and I felt dizzy. The bag fell out of my hand and the glass clattered on the ground. Shaken, I lifted my head and saw a huge van had parked on the drive and its shadow blotted out the sunlight. I told myself wrong house, three point turn, they will go in a minute, it is an omen, a sign to tell me to take a break. Better have a cup of tea. I'll feel stronger after a cuppa.

About to open the kitchen door I heard someone yell. "Freddy!"

I couldn't be sure but I thought I recognised the voice, I smiled and without looking yelled, "Hey Granddad!"

Angry and relieved at the same time, thinking I'm glad to see him but should tell him off, I didn't know what to say. He was back and there was nothing more important. We could have a cup of tea and a chat, see what he had been doing and I could tell I missed him and… No I wouldn't tell him I nearly mixed the glass and cardboard. There was no need to make a fuss, it wouldn't make any difference, so I shouted, "Come on! Have a cup of tea?"

"The new way or the old way?" he asked with a grin.

I sighed, he hadn't changed, the same old Granddad, "Your way" I said. "Definitely your way!"

"Same old Freddy" he said. "Did you notice the van?"

The van, the shadow that blotted out the sun and made me think I had passed out, "No I didn't notice" I lied, "I expect whoever drove it here will take it away. There isn't room for such a big thing on my drive. I'm sure they will go soon".

"Well, I will move it soon" Granddad said, "after a cuppa!"

He hadn't actually said the van was his but it certainly sounded like he meant it. "Are you trying to tell me that is your van Granddad. You can't drive!"

He held up a driving licence, pointed to the photo and proudly announced, "Mine!" The thing had his name on it and the photo resembled him without a hat.

He used to wobble on a bike and had never driven anything except the Dust Wagon, until Speedy let him drive that wonderful electric car. Reminded of that day I sighed, "Well done" but found it hard to believe he had passed his test in a few short months. He had some explaining to do.

Sitting on his stool, minding a cup of tea, Granddad began his explanation. "Speedy gave me a driving lesson. I've had a few more, passed my driving test and bought the van. It is the Recycling Van and I am the Recycling Man ready to serve the Recycling Army". Granddad had a mission in mind, and sounding more serious than I'd ever heard, he told me he wants to do anything he can to stop Global Warming, and recycling helps. **He insisted, "There is no need to make more plastic or mine for more aluminium or make more glass! Make better use of what we have. There is lots of it. We need it to be recycled!"**

His outburst surprised and worried me, getting excited might give him a heart attack. I told him to calm down.

Calmly he said, "You have been teaching me about recycling. When you were a youngster you learned to make the most of what we had and I know you understand. We can do this!"

He had been my inspiration, my teacher, my example, I looked up to him. I am what I am because he taught me and when he said I understand I felt humble. Qualifications, success, achievements never made me feel the way I felt at that moment. I'd never felt so special.

He hadn't explained what he meant by Recycling Man but I felt concerned that he might want me to be involved. We would have to talk to people about recycling and there may be forms to fill in. I hate filling in forms and not qualified to tell people what to do. I protested, "This is England and you can't just get up and get busy, there is mountains of paperwork and things. You are not qualified, and what about form filling?"

Holding up his new driving licence he responded brightly, "Ready, willing and able, and you can do them".

I didn't want to do them. Wriggling, hoping to find a way to avoid any involvement without being positively negative, in fact sort of humouring him, I asked, "Have you got any customers?"

"Lots" he said enthusiastically, "200 little businesses in town have signed up. They can't wait to get started!"

I should have congratulated him but didn't. Gobsmacked, I didn't know what to say.

Still searching for an excuse to stay at home I asked, "How can you afford to do this?"

"It will pay! It's all in Roy's blue print, his plan shows businesses don't collect recycling, they throw everything in the khaki bin because they have to pay too much for Recycling Management, and they don't want to pay".

I seized the opportunity to find a way out and said, "Are you sure they want to? If they don't want to pay Recycling Management why should they pay you?"

Carefully Granddad gave his reason. "They do want to. They don't want to pay too much! I had to find a price they will pay. Do you know most little businesses drive their waste to the Tip themselves?"

He didn't know the Council have renamed it. I told him, "It is called the Recycling Centre, Granddad, not the Tip".

Granddad had always called it the Tip or the Dump. He grinned and told me, "The trip to the Tip costs money so I convinced them they will save time and money if they let me manage the waste. I've worked it all out".

He had gone to a lot of trouble, buying a van, doing working out, he clearly wanted to be the Recycling Man. I hoped he had done his sums right, but doubted it, and thought about problems like, he might have forgotten to wear his glasses and missed a decimal point. A decimal point in the wrong place can make pounds into pence, profit into loss, success into failure. I needed more information. Using my best psychology I praised him, "Granddad, you are amazing!"

He wanted to share the praise, with Roy, and hastily told me it is all in his plan. "It is Roy's idea. It's in his blue print. All I had to do was follow his instructions, do the calculations and make a small…"

I interrupted eagerly, "Fortune!"

"Profit" Granddad corrected. "My biggest problem will be jealous management people who think I'm stealing their business, but I'm not. My customers never had any management. These people want to hand in recycling but have never been able to. They can't afford it".

Earlier I asked how much he would charge and he didn't tell me, so I asked, "What fees do the competition charge? What do small businesses think is too much, and what do they think is just right?"

He made it obvious he was not going to tell me by disregarding the question and rather like Melon he seemed to be saying on the one hand and then on the other. In the conversation with himself he muttered, "Council is a big business and gives big businesses big bins, I am a small business and I'll give small businesses small ones…" He stopped then added, "Unless they want big ones".

He looked up and suddenly began explaining how it would work. I realised why he had avoided telling me before. It was very complicated. One pound here, two pounds there, electric versus petrol. The customers must put the good stuff in his bin and the rubbish in the Council's. He finally said, "Roy is sure they will do their best, especially if it saves them money. I'm relying on them. Isn't that right Freddy?"

I could tell his intentions were good. Although I usually like to hear something twice to make sure I understand, my head was like a case full of figures, I couldn't get any more in. He had considered everything and confused me but I had to agree. "Yes, Granddad, if they spend two pounds on petrol to drive cardboard to the Recycling Centre and you take it to be recycled and only charge one pound they will get the recycling done and save money".

He didn't comment but looked at the kitchen clock and said, "Time races on. I bet you want to take a look at the van. Come on, I'll show you".

I followed, eager to see the van that cast a huge shadow over me earlier, Granddad's Recycling Van. It was like a long, tall motor home. It made me smile. We walked slowly from one end to the other admiring the clean white paintwork, commenting on its shiny newness.

"Electric" Granddad said, "None of that smelly petrol stuff, but you might smell the tyres, they are rubber".

"Of course they are," I mocked, "and I suppose you're going to tell me the wheels are round".

For a moment I stopped to admire his van and imagined a motor home like no other, fitted with luxuries, things I like but can't afford. On the floor in every room, wall to wall pure wool, air soft carpets, in the lounge a faux mink three-piece suite, in the dining room oak table and chairs and the kitchen better than mine. Hanging over the dining room and lounge two mezzanine bedrooms with four poster beds. The sort I'd seen in a Grand Homes magazine. Probably fitted with central heating too.

Granddad bounced up the steps to the door and invited me to look inside. I had imagined it would be like something I'd never seen, I was right. It had been modified to be a Recycling Van. The first thing that struck me was the vast emptiness and equipment. I gasped “A conveyor, a baler, a bin and nothing else. It’s a mini MRF. It reminds me of the Tardis”.

Granddad grinned his false teeth grin and said, “Great! Isn’t it. We can do sorting on the move. That small bin is for the rubbish. I hope we never ever fill it. If our customers do the job properly and sort the good stuff for us we never will”.

I asked him to explain what he meant by sorting on the move.

“No need to sit about doing nothing” he said. “You can always be sorting and I can be driving. If there are any problems we can talk about them between customers. You’ll love it, and when you are not busy you can come and sit in the front, with me”.

“How very thoughtful, I do like to sit down sometimes” I said sarcastically.

Granddad ignored my sarcasm and insisted, “You will love the passenger seat, your seat, and the modified dash board, Freddy. I had it all done with you in mind”.

Secretly impressed and pleased with the mini MRF inside the cargo space the usual van seat and dash would be adequate, but I had to see the cab and my chair. It appeared to be an arm chair and he wanted me to try it, so I did. It was the most comfortable chair I had ever sat on. To the side there was a pen holder, a laptop tray, and the all important cup holder and cup. This would be my favourite chair and I would never want to sit anywhere else.

“Do you like the dash board?” Granddad asked and watched my surprise. It looked ridiculously complicated. Sets of instruments resembling a navigation system in an aeroplane and an array of buttons, switches and dials that seemed to show everything from the weather to the route, a big screen with internet connection for radio, television and

Global Positioning, a GPS unit that gives the position of the van wherever it goes, it had everything.

Sitting back and relaxing in my chair I said, "This is the life, It is more comfortable than any I have at home. You wont be able to get me out of it. I'll sit here all day".

Pleased, Granddad said, "Glad you like it. Told you I had it done with you in mind. It is a great place to keep an eye on the dash".

I thought, the dash is the sort of thing drivers keep an eye on, not passengers. I would look out of the window at the street, pedestrians, and even over the tops of cars into the distance, no need to watch the dash. My view changed when he said, "If I get this wrong we might fly".

Suddenly watching the dash became very important. One of the many dash lights beamed brightly and Granddad said, "Engine running. Can you hear it?"

I listened then said, "It is so quiet. I'll need a stethoscope to hear it. Is it electric?"

Granddad grinned. He confirmed it was electric and proudly told me no one would hear it and on a nice sunny day the wheels barely touch the ground so there will not be a lot of road noise.

I stared, admiring him, thinking my Granddad's idea and his van were amazing. He was going to make an effort to save the Planet. Speaking with a lump in my throat I said, "Granddad you are fantastic!"

He never liked praise and I worked out why. He did what he thought was right and didn't need anything for doing it.

All at once I realised the van was rolling down the drive, towards the high street. I panicked and screamed "The van is moving backwards. Where are we going? I've seen everything and heard all I need to hear. We don't need to go for a drive".

The van continued to roll out on to the road and Granddad handed me a list. "Customers!" He called out, "This is our Card Day. Hold on! We will collect cardboard from all those customers".

I called out the first name on the list. He called back, "No need to tell me. The on-board computer knows it all. When we get near it will say the name, address and weight of card to pick up".

Amazed I said, "Will it? How will it do that?"

Confidently Granddad told me he did an Artificial Intelligence (AI) crash course and designed a computer program. The on-board computer talks to all the customers bins. When we pick up the good waste from a customer the computer gathers all the information and sends messages to printers to print out certificates.

Crash course, computer program, all too clever for me, I didn't take it in. "Run that by me again, Granddad, I don't think I understand".

"You do, you just don't know it," Granddad laughed, and pointed to the dash. "Everything is done in there, except the printer is in your office at home. By the time we have finished collecting all our card your printer will have printed out two hundred certificates for us. Each customer can print out their own".

The van stopped and Granddad pointed to the screen on the dash and told me to look. The screen showed the bins outside Minnie Macs computer store, owner Alan Clever and a weight of cardboard to be collected.

This had to be the easiest job in the world. We had driven into the high street, stopped at the first customer and now the customer was going to push good waste card onto the van. "I like this" I said, "it is incredible, brilliant, I can't believe it! You have created an app that will do all this!"

Granddad smiled with pride, "Yes, all you have to do now is lift the card on board and give the bins back".

"Me?" I whined, "I have to lift all that card onto the van. How much is there?"

"You work out!" Granddad said. "What can you lift?"

"A few" I moaned, "hundred kilos or so".

"No one will have a hundred kilos so you can lift it. He has five bins and only 5 kilos in each one. Come on I'll give you a hand".

Granddad meant he would chat to Alan while they watched me do the lifting but it wasn't too bad.

Granddad asked "Do you want to do the driving or sorting, Freddy?" He then said, "You are in the back so it will be easier if you do the sorting. If you want the conveyor to run just push the button on the side. The big red one! Remember to push it! The computer wont do everything".

I know, I said to myself, that's why I have to do the lifting and sorting.

At the fifth customer I complained Granddad was driving too fast. I needed his help to do the sorting and didn't know how to operate the baler. I asked him to stop. He was extremely pleased with our progress, said we were ahead of schedule and suggested he would stop and help at every fifth customer. I wanted to tell him I hated it and wanted to stop for ever but I didn't and very soon began to enjoy the perks of the job; listening to music while I worked, stopping every few minutes for a break and occasionally chatting to the customers.

CHAPTER 16

On the way home, sitting in my very comfortable passenger seat, I listened to Granddad rave about how well we had done. He didn't notice how loud he sounded until I reminded him the van is electric, very quiet and he didn't need to shout.

Still enthusiastic but quieter he reviewed what we had done. He gave the impression we had finished and asked for my thoughts. I had baled all the cardboard into small blocks and my home printer should have printed hundreds of certificates. I told him when we get home, he can make the tea while I file the certificates and off-load all the mini bales. I said, "We will have to compress them together to make big blocks. Where is the big baler?"

If he had told me before I would have insisted it would not be possible to put a baler in the back garden, but it was too late. We had come this far and the way he said, "In the back garden, Freddy" made it sound obvious. I could not argue, so repeated his words comically, "In the back garden Freddy" and added, "As if I didn't know".

He smiled, almost laughed, as he said, "Of course you did". He commented the rubbish bin in the van was empty and claimed his good, well trained, customers only put good clean cardboard in their bins. When I asked what he would do with their rubbish he replied curtly, he would have to get a special bin for it.

Thinking ahead Granddad said, "Tomorrow we will do aluminium. I like aluminium, don't you? We will bale it and the fun size blocks will look nice in the garden".

"I used to like aluminium" I said grudgingly, "but I don't need blocks of it all over my garden!"

"You'll get used to them, and the glass and plastic. You'll be able to have a garden open day, let everyone see the wonderful art. They may wish to donate to good causes, improving the environment, stopping global warming, reducing emissions and you might have a spot on TV".

I thought, Granddad's sense of humour doesn't change.

Next morning he knocked on the door. I opened it in my Picker gear. He chanted, "Have you emptied the van? We have cans to collect, today is aluminium Can Day. Pubs, clubs, cafes that sort of place, not so many customers, just lots of cans".

More familiar with the process, I knew the on-board computer would speak but I still jumped when the very clever thing spoke. It had talked to the customers waste bins and poured lots of information into its memory banks and told me and Granddad everything it knew. "Club one," it said, "Kenny Clarke, aluminium, one hundred kilograms, ready to pick up".

Alarm bells rang in my head as I imagined an enormous bin filled with millions of cans, too many, impossible to lift. I protested "I can't lift all them! I can lift a hundred kilograms but not in a bin twice as big as me!"

Granddad gave me some important information that soothed me. "I've thought of that. Kenny has lots of small bins so he can climb in and do the squash dance. I'm sure you'll have no trouble handling squashed cans".

At the road side I saw Kenny waving beside lots of small bins. Thankfully he lifted them onto the van and I filled the hopper. I asked, "Have you done the squash dance? You know jumped on the bins and…" Kenny's puzzled look told me he had no idea what I was talking about. I said, "You haven't, have you?"

He had a good sense of humour and replied, "You're joking. I've seen all sorts of dances in the club but never the squash dance. I guess if you show the youngsters how to do it they'll try".

"It is more of an older person dance" I said, "Granddad is very good at it, but he is good at everything, and excels at watching me do all the work".

We worked steadily. Kenny lifted the full bins onto the van. I poured the cans into the hopper and gave him the empties back. The whole operation flowed so well, it felt professional. Kenny didn't know how many customers we had and neither did I so when he said, "You must have lots of customers, I'm number one thousand and one". I answered modestly, "One or two".

He told me he and his team had been trained by Granddad and praised him. "Granddad knows what he is doing. He's had lots of experience, professionally trained. He showed me and my team to sort recycling properly. We separate the good from the bad. We are all keen to do it his way. You wont find any rubbish in MY BINS". I had not noticed till then each bin had My Bin, written on the side, I guessed Granddad decided that name would give people a sense of ownership and make them proud to do the best recycling possible.

He counted each bin and as he lifted the final one onto the van said, "That wasn't too bad. That is the last one".

"That's good," I said, "must press on, lots to do. We will be back".

Granddad had fooled Kenny. Everything he knows he learned in a few days in my kitchen and a few days picking. He passed that on to Kenny and the other customers. Kenny thought we had thousands of customers and he had been trained to separate good from bad, by a recycling expert. He didn't know yesterday was our first Card Day and today our first Aluminium Day. In my head I calculated Kenny had paid Granddad a collection fee and all those cans would be worth a hundred pounds to someone, and even though I wasn't sure who, I recited Granddad's favourite saying, where there's muck there's money. The job will pay, and it is made easy because the van's Very Intelligent Computer (VIC) knows everything. It talks to the customer's bins and knows how much is in them. We arrive, do our collection and the computer notes everything and sends all the information to my home printer.

As for me, I collect the recycling, load the hopper, push the conveyor button and pick out the rubbish, if there is any. When there is ten kilograms in the baler the conveyor stops, the baler squashes its load, makes a cube, I empty it and push the button again.

Granddad heard my conversation with Kenny and when I joined him in the cab commented, "Customer number, one thousand and one likes to chat and be helpful. I wonder if you could have handled all the bins without him? Some customers will not lift one bin. Could you manage on your own?"

I couldn't complain, but thought, it is his business and I'm practically doing it all. The only thing I haven't done is drive.

Before we set off he asked if I would like to.

Without hesitation I replied, "Of course! I thought you would never ask" and raced to sit in the driving seat. Rushing and excitement made me hyperventilate. For a moment I felt dizzy and the buttons and switches floated aimlessly across the dashboard. My eyes were not focussing so I felt with my feet for the pedals. One was missing. In panic I said, "I can't find the clutch pedal!"

Unconcerned Granddad told me, "It is automatic. It doesn't need a clutch pedal, Freddy. Be calm and breath!"

A few deep breaths later my vision cleared, I was ready to go. Holding the steering wheel and pressing the accelerator the van took us to the next customer. I jumped at the synthesised Granddad voice saying, "You are approaching Harry What's Wine Bar, here you will collect …" and I stopped the van beside another dozen bins.

"Mind you don't hit them" Granddad said anxiously, "you're very close. Harry is another chatty one so this could take some time".

Harry did help, he lifted while I emptied. This recycling is so easy, I told myself, and the customers are nice. I didn't think I would like the job but I do. I must thank Granddad for setting it up.

Driving home, feeling like a professional Waste Manager, I thought I can't keep piling all the mini bales in my garden so asked Granddad what he is going to do with them?

With his usual calm approach he said, "Don't worry, Freddy, it's all sorted".

Thinking he was being funny I said, "I know! I sorted it! I mean when we get home, what are you going to do with them?"

"Oh!" he laughed, "I had a word with Joe. Speedy will collect them and squash them into big bales. They will sell them and we can share the profit".

Stunned, I said, "Did you do that? We are going to make some money. The businesses pay us to collect their recycling waste and MRF are going to pay us too. That is amazing! Someone once said recycling doesn't pay, they were wrong. It does. Granddad you are a genius".

As always modest he said, "Thanks Freddy".

We emptied the mini bales ready for Speedy then had a cup of tea.

I had mine in the Recycle Angel cup, Granddad insisted, and before he left he joked, "Just remember to be ready for Speedy in the morning. I will be polishing my halo".

Speedy arrived nice and early to pick up the mini bales. He asked if Granddad was going to help. I told him he said he would be polishing his halo. Speedy laughed and told me Granddad is a Business Angel. He set up Recycle Angel for me and was about to set up another for a friend.

I wanted to know how he had done it. Speedy said Granddad told Joe he wanted to start a mobile Recycling Business and needed driving lessons, a van and somewhere to sell the recyclables he collected. Joe told him to give Granddad driving lessons and Joe helped with the van and said if he brought clean mini bales he would sell them and share the profit.

When he passed his driving test Sammy gave him a good reference and helped him to get customers. He couldn't have done it without them.

Granddad had moved on, he was polishing his halo helping set up another Recycle Angel business. I guessed he would drop in from time to time but there is a lot of recycling to do.

About Fred Page

"I think we are at a point where we don't want to accept the consequences of our actions. Many people believe that 'recycling doesn't work' so I decided to check. I met the recycling team manager and learned of some of the problems they face. I also searched the Internet to find out what happens to the recycling we put in the bin. Not restricted by imposed rule, I wrote the story"

Fred is retired and lives in the North East of England. He has a passion for writing and is looking forward to future literary projects. Fred is ethically concerned and a keen supporter of reducing carbon emissions and stopping waste being dumped in the seas and oceans.

Copyright © 2021 by Fred Page

Printed in Great Britain
by Amazon

72239277R00081